BATMAN DETECTIVE COMICS

VOL. 2

FEAR STATE

MARIKO TAMAKI
DAN WATTERS | MATTHEW ROSENBERG
writers

DAN MORA | DAVID LAPHAM | VIKTOR BOGDANOVIC
MAX RAYNOR | DARICK ROBERTSON
pencillers

DAN MORA | DAVID LAPHAM | DANIEL HENRIQUES | VIKTOR BOGDANOVIC
MAX RAYNOR | DARICK ROBERTSON
inkers

BATMAN

JORDIE BELLAIRE | TRISH MULVIHILL | ARIF PRIANTO | DIEGO RODRIGUEZ
colorists

ADITYA BIDIKAR | ROB LEIGH
letterers

DAN MORA
collection cover artist

Batman created by
BOB KANE with BILL FINGER

DETECTIVE COMICS

VOL. 2

FEAR STATE

Paul Kaminski
Editor – Original Series
Dave Wielgosz
Associate Editor – Original Series
Steve Buccellato and Paul Kaminski
Editors – Collected Edition
Steve Cook
Design Director – Books
Megen Bellersen
Publication Design
Erin Vanover
Publication Production

Marie Javins
Editor-in-Chief, DC Comics

Anne DePies
Senior VP – General Manager
Jim Lee
Publisher & Chief Creative Officer
Don Falletti
VP – Manufacturing Operations & Workflow Management
Lawrence Ganem
VP – Talent Services
Alison Gill
Senior VP – Manufacturing & Operations
Jeffrey Kaufman
VP – Editorial Strategy & Programming
Nick J. Napolitano
VP – Manufacturing Administration & Design
Nancy Spears
VP – Revenue

BATMAN: DETECTIVE COMICS VOL. 2: FEAR STATE

DC Comics, 2900 West Alameda Ave., Burbank, CA 91505
Printed by Transcontinental Interglobe, Beauceville, QC, Canada.
5/27/22. First Printing. ISBN: 978-1-77951-555-1

Library of Congress Cataloging-in-Publication Data is available.

PEFC Certified
This product is from sustainably managed forests and controlled sources
PEFC
PEFC/01-31-106
www.pefc.org

DETECTIVE COMICS #1040

cover by DAN MORA

GCPD. MIDTOWN PRECINCT.
GOTHAM CITY POLICE DEPARTMENT
WORST VACATION OF MY LIFE.
THIS CITY IS $#@%.
THE STREETS ARE $#@%. YOU GUYS ARE $#@%.
NEVER AGAIN.
ALL I WANT TO KNOW IS--
--WHAT ARE YOU DOING ABOUT THE GUY WHO STOLE MY CAR?
YOU CAME TO GOTHAM CITY FOR A VACATION?
YOU THINK THIS IS FUNNY?
THAT'S IT. I'M CALLING THE CITY COUNCILLOR.
GO FOR IT.
EXCUSE ME.
I WAS BEING HELD IN CUSTODY AT THE FORT GRAYE PRECINCT BEFORE IT WAS...ER, BLOWN UP.*
*AND HOW! IN DETECTIVE COMICS #1037. --PK
OH! UH...JUST A SECOND.
HEY, UH, IS THAT--?
ENJOY THE REST OF YOUR VACATION.
"BRUCE WAYNE ESCAPED? HE WAS IN JAIL?"

WE HAD HIM IN FOR QUESTIONING FOR THE WORTH CASE.
I THOUGHT WE RELEASED HIM.
EXIT
WE DIDN'T. SO GET THE INVESTIGATORS ON THE LINE AND FIND OUT WHAT THEY WANT US TO DO.
MEANTIME...
...PUT HIM IN THE TANK. WORST HE'LL GET IS PUKE ON HIS SUIT WHILE WE FIGURE THIS OUT.
FRIDAY NIGHT. WON'T GET OUT UNTIL SUNDAY IF HE'S LUCKY.
HE'LL LIVE.
"BRUCE. TURNING YOURSELF IN, WHAT DOES THAT ACHIEVE?"
"I CAN'T HAVE THE COPS CHASING BRUCE WAYNE FOR SARAH'S AND LYDIA'S MURDERS, AND BATMAN FOR EVERYTHING ELSE."

"SO YOU GO TO THE STATION. I'LL MAKE SURE THE POLICE PUT THE PIECES TOGETHER ON THE WORTH MURDER SO BRUCE CAN WALK OUT AND WALK AWAY."
"MUCH APPRECIATED, ORACLE."
OKAY, BARBARA.
LET'S PULL TOGETHER THIS CASE FOR GOTHAM'S DETECTIVES SO WE CAN GET BRUCE WAYNE OUT OF JAIL.
LOOK AT THAT. IT'S ALL RIGHT HERE. FOOTAGE. TIME STAMP. EASY-PEASY.
DEET
TIME TO CHECK IN ON OUR PATIENTS.
DEET
HEY, JENNIFER. HOW ARE THEY?
HELENA BERTINELLI AND DEB DONOVAN WERE BOTH CLEARED OF THEIR INFECTIONS.
LAST BLOOD SAMPLES JUST CAME IN AND LOOK GREAT.
EXCELLENT. THANKS FOR CHECKING.
ANYTIME, BARBARA.

SPEAKING OF, LET'S SEE IF THEY'RE AWAKE.
HELLO THERE. HOW ARE WE FEELING?
HEY! YOU GOT ANYTHING TO EAT THAT'S NOT PUDDING?
WAIT...
WHAT HAPPENED TO THE WOMAN IN THIS BED?
I GUESS SHE CHECKED OUT.*
WITH MY COAT, FOR WHAT IT'S WORTH.
*FOLLOW HUNTRESS'S ADVENTURE IN BATMAN SECRET FILES: HUNTRESS #1, ON SALE NOW! --PK
SEEMED LIKE SHE WAS IN A HURRY.
&%@#.

"HEY. BARBARA? UPDATE. HELENA IS M.I.A. OKAY. OUT THE WINDOW, I THINK."
HEY, MAN, IS IT FRIDAY?
IT'S SATURDAY.
CRAP.
HEY.
HELLO.
YOU KNOW WHAT I KNOW?
WHAT?
YOU'RE BRUCE WAYNE.
YES. I AM.
RRRRRIGHT.
YOU KNOW WHAT ELSE I KNOW?
WHAT'S THAT?

YOU'RE BATMAN.
BATMAN?
...HOW DO YOU FIGURE THAT?
HEH HEH.
LIKE FIVE YEARS AGO? LIKE A LOT OF YEARS AGO? MAYBE NOT THAT MANY YEARS AGO...
JACKY PIZZA
"...I WAS WORKING IN ENTERTAINMENT THEN. VERY TAXING GIG. SO I WAS UNWINDING ONE NIGHT.
KRASCH
"STUFF WAS ALWAYS HAPPENING AROUND THEN. STUFF THAT MEANT A PERSON SHOULDN'T BE OUT ON THE STREET TOO LATE.
"YOU KNOW..."

"GOTHAM STUFF."

"SO I RUN, RIGHT?
"ALTHOUGH WHO KNOWS WHERE TO RUN IN THESE SITUATIONS.
"I THINK MY PLAN WAS TO GO GET TO HIGHER GROUND.
"FIRE ESCAPES ARE HARDER TO JUMP ON THAN YOU THINK.
"MOVIES ALWAYS MAKE THAT STUFF LOOK SO EASY.
"ANYWAY...
"BEHIND ME, I COULD HEAR THAT THINGS WERE GETTING REAL.
"IT WAS BATMAN AND THE JOKER. THOSE GUYS GET INTO IT, Y'KNOW?"

"YEAH, ONE OF THE SCARIER NIGHTS OF MY LIFE.
"I DON'T KNOW, I LOOKED TO SEE IF IT WAS IN THE PAPERS THE NEXT DAY, I THINK.
"MAYBE IT WAS. I MIGHTA FORGOT.
"SO THEN THERE'S, LIKE... QUIET. EXCEPT I CAN STILL HEAR MY HEART BEATING LIKE A FRICKIN' DRUM.
"ALL THAT CLIMBING. I WAS ABOUT TO PASS OUT. JUST...TIRED.
"THAT'S WHEN I REALIZE...WHEN I HEAR IT..."

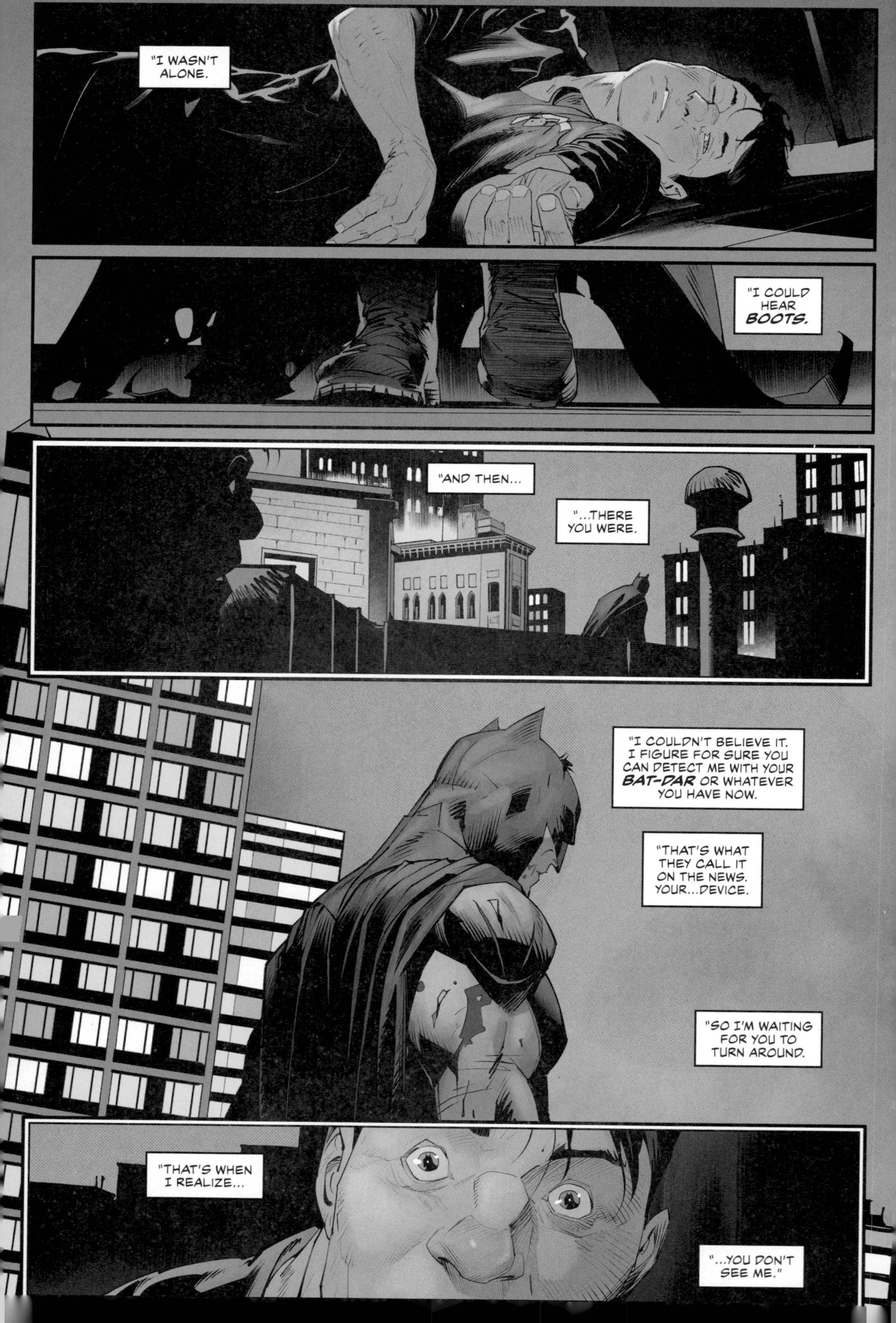
"I WASN'T ALONE.
"I COULD HEAR BOOTS.
"AND THEN...
"...THERE YOU WERE.
"I COULDN'T BELIEVE IT. I FIGURE FOR SURE YOU CAN DETECT ME WITH YOUR BAT-DAR OR WHATEVER YOU HAVE NOW.
"THAT'S WHAT THEY CALL IT ON THE NEWS. YOUR...DEVICE.
"SO I'M WAITING FOR YOU TO TURN AROUND.
"THAT'S WHEN I REALIZE...
"...YOU DON'T SEE ME."

"YOU HAD SOMETHING IN YOUR EYE."
"YOU'RE SURE OF WHAT YOU SAW?"
"I'M NOT SURE OF ANYTHING, MAN."

I LIVE IN GOTHAM CITY. I GOT A SISTER WHO THINKS SHE'S GONNA MARRY BAT-WOMAN. YOU KNOW? BUT. IT MAKES SENSE, RIGHT? THAT YOU WOULD BE BATMAN.
WHY?
BECAUSE I READ THE PAPERS. HORRIBLE THINGS HAPPEN TO YOU. AND YOU SEEM LIKE THE KIND OF GUY WHO'D MAKE IT SO THAT HORRIBLE THINGS KEEP HAPPENING TO YOU.
THAT'S HOW YOU SEE IT.
TAKES ONE TO KNOW ONE.
WELL...
YOU NEED HIS ADDRESS? OKAY. YEAH, NOT WAYNE MANOR. HEH. UPTOWN, THOUGH.

THE ICEBERG LOUNGE.
OFFICE OF OSWALD COBBLEPOT.
ALL RIGHT. THANK YOU.
WHO'S UP FOR A LITTLE *DELIVERY?*
A LITTLE SASHIMI?
THEN AFTER DINNER, WE BURN SOMETHING DOWN.

GOTHAM CITY POLICE DEPARTMENT
OKAY, EVERYONE UP! LOOK ALIVE! IT'S NOT A HOTEL.
WHAT THE &@#$ DIFFERENCE DOES IT MAKE IF WE'RE ASLEEP?
IT'S MONDAY. THEY'RE LETTING US OUT.
*&%$, MY &%$@# HEAD. WHERE THE HELL AM I?
CAN I HELP YOU, BUDDY?
BUDDY?
LOOK, MAN. IT'S BEEN A LONG NIGHT. SORRY FOR WHATEVER I SAID, OKAY? DON'T TAKE IT PERSONALLY.
IS IT SUNDAY OR MONDAY?
MONDAY.
*&$%.
BRUCE WAYNE. LET'S GO!

NICE MEETING YOU.
YEAH, YOU TOO, BUDDY.
APOLOGIES FOR THE INCONVENIENCE, MR. WAYNE. THE ALIBI YOU PROVIDED CHECKED OUT. WE'LL BE IN TOUCH WITH ANY FURTHER QUESTIONS.
SURE THING. WHATEVER YOU NEED.
"I'M HAPPY TO HELP.
WEEEEEEEEEE
DAMN...

GOTHAM CITY SHIPYARD.
I'M A BUSY MAN, PENGUIN.
SPEAK.
VILE IS ALIVE.
HOW ALIVE?

ALIVE ENOUGH.
ALIVE ENOUGH THAT OUR AGREEMENT, OUR PLAN, MAY GO FORWARD.
HMPH.
BRUCE WAYNE WILL DIE.
YES. YES HE WILL.

THIS TERRIBLE CITY. WHAT A SHAME.
BARK! BARK!
"PLANS FOR WAYNE'S VIOLENT DEATH ARE ALREADY UNDER WAY. BUT AS WE AGREED EARLIER, MR. WORTH..."

...IF WE ARE TO DO THIS EFFECTIVELY, WE NEED TO CUT OFF WAYNE'S PROTECTION, FULLY.
AND SO BATMAN...
...WILL BE OUR FIRST PRIORITY.
"THEN WE WILL SERVE YOU BRUCE WAYNE'S BEATING HEART ON A SILVER PLATTER."

WITH THIS MONSTER, WE'LL HAVE ALL WE NEED...
...TO DESTROY BATMAN.
THE JURY HAS SPOKEN.
The WEEKENDER
MARIKO TAMAKI Writer DAN MORA Artist
JORDIE BELLAIRE Colors ADITYA BIDIKAR Letters
DAN MORA Cover LEE BERMEJO Variant Cover
DAVE WIELGOSZ Associate Editor
PAUL KAMINSKI Editor BEN ABERNATHY Group Editor
BATMAN created by BOB KANE with BILL FINGER
NEXT: WE THE JURY

"I CAN HEAR THEM.
I CAN HEAR THEIR VICTIMS CRYING FOR HELP."

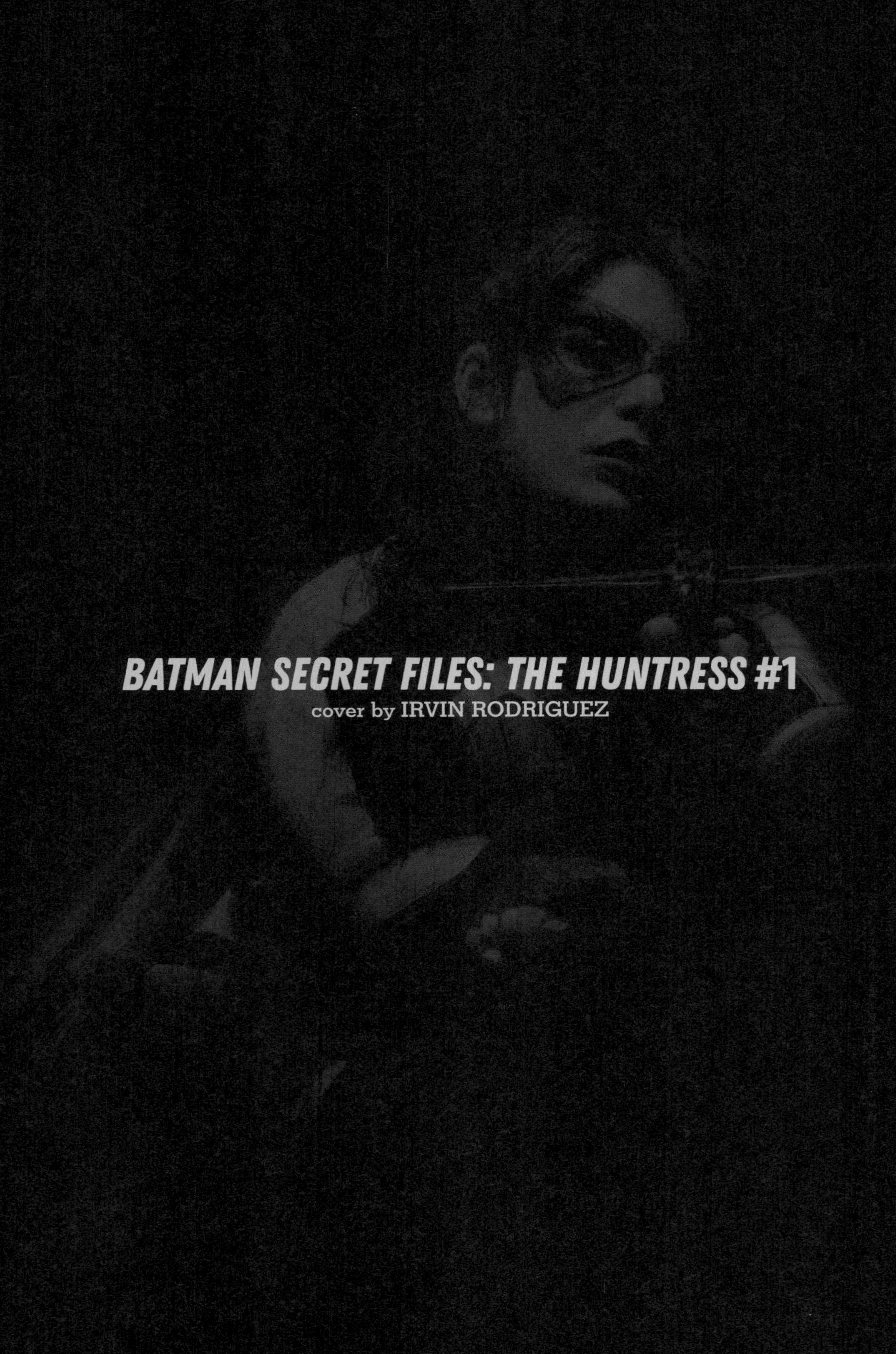

BATMAN SECRET FILES: THE HUNTRESS #1

cover by IRVIN RODRIGUEZ

RATTLE
CRRREEEEAAAAKKK
RROW?
HUNTRESS
IN
SEE YOU
I'M HOME.
THUNK
MARIKO TAMAKI
writer
DAVID LAPHAM
artist
TRISH MULVIHILL
colors
ROB LEIGH
letters
IRVIN RODRIGUEZ
cover
RICCARDO FEDERICI
variant cover
DAVE WIELGOSZ
associate editor
PAUL KAMINSKI
editor
BEN ABERNATHY
group editor

HEY, DOUG.
OOF.
I'M FINE, THANKS. I'LL BE FINE.
I JUST NEED TO PULL THIS THING--
--OUT OF MY ARM.
PAT
Guh.
GROSS.
WHAT DID THE NURSE SAY? I'M DEHYDRATED?
WHY DON'T I JUST LIE HERE FOR A SECOND?
I CAN UPDATE YOU ON MY ADVENTURES.
"I WAS HELPING BATMAN THROUGH A SERIES OF HIS MESSES.
"AGAIN.
"SOME %&#?!$@ BLEW UP THE ENTIRE CITY SEWER SYSTEM."

"I TRACKED DOWN HUE VILE, THE EPICENTER OF A PARASITIC FLASH MOB OF VIOLENCE IN GOTHAM.*
CAUTION
*AS SEEN IN RECENT ISSUES OF DETECTIVE COMICS-- WHICH CULMINATED IN THIS SCENE FROM #1039! --PAUL
"HE INFECTED ME.
"I STABBED HIM.
"DON'T KNOW IF YOU'VE EVER BEEN INFECTED BY A RABID BRAIN PARASITE.
"I DO NOT RECOMMEND IT.
"LIKE BEING SUFFOCATED INSIDE YOUR OWN BRAIN.
"I KNEW IT WAS HIM, IT WAS VILE, HOLDING ME DOWN.
"UNDERWATER."

YEEESSSSSSSS
"I COULD FEEL MY BODY *MOVING,* SOMEWHERE ABOVE THE SURFACE, JUST OUT OF REACH.
"I MEAN, LOOK, HAVE I WANTED TO DECK BATMAN BEFORE? *SURE.*
"BUT IT'S SOMETHING *ELSE* TO FEEL YOUR HANDS REACHING FOR SOMEONE'S *THROAT...*
"...BECAUSE SOMETHING INSIDE YOU...WHICH ISN'T YOU BUT FEELS LIKE IT'S TAKEN UP ALL THE SPACE THAT *IS* YOU... WANTS TO HEAR THEIR SPINE *CRACK.*
"LIKE WHEN YOU'RE A KID AND SOMEONE SCREAMS AND THAT SCREAM IS ALL YOU CAN HEAR.
"VILE'S *RAGE* WAS ALL I COULD HEAR.
"AND THEN..."

"...I WOKE UP IN WHAT I'M ASSUMING WAS AN *OUT-OF-HEALTH-PLAN* HOSPITAL BED.
I NEED TO GET OUT OF HERE.
YOU'RE LUCKY. WE CLEARED THE PARASITE.
I *NEED* TO GET *OUT* OF HERE.
YOU'RE *DEHYDRATED.*
I'VE BEEN WORSE.
I HEARD YOU TRIED TO MURDER BATMAN.
I-- WHO--
DEB DONOVAN. I *ALSO* TRIED TO MURDER BATMAN.
I'M A REPORTER.
NOT THAT THAT'S WHY I TRIED TO MURDER HIM.
"I GOT OUT OF THERE AS SOON AS I COULD STAND UP WITHOUT BARFING.
DID THAT @&#$& TAKE MY COAT?
"TWENTY BLOCKS IN A TRENCH COAT AND A HOSPITAL GOWN LATER..."

I'M HOME. I FEEL LIKE @&#%.
WE STILL DON'T KNOW WHO VILE IS OR WHERE HE CAME FROM.
OR HOW MANY HE INFECTED WITH HIS RAGE WORMS THAT TURN PEOPLE INTO CARNIVOROUS KILLING-MACHINE PUPPETS.
BUT AT LEAST WHATEVER HE DID TO MY BRAIN IS GONE.
I JUST NEED SOME NOT-IN-THE-HOSPITAL SLEEP.
JUST A LITTLE SLEEP. THEN I'LL--
HNNNNNNN...
UHN...

MEEAR!
WHAT?
IS THIS...
...A NIGHTMARE?
HOW CAN THIS BE A NIGHTMARE, IF MY EYES ARE OPEN?
HOW IS IT A NIGHTMARE IF I CAN SEE THE SWEAT ON HIS FACE?

OKAY, HELENA. TAKE A BREATH.
PARASITE'S GONE. THIS IS A FLASHBACK.
SPLASH SPLASH
SPLASHHH
TYPICAL SUPERHERO-TRAUMA-AFTERMATH STUFF.
EXCEPT HOW IS IT A FLASHBACK IF I'M LOOKING AT A PERSON...
MFFFF...
...I'VE NEVER SEEN BEFORE?
Pant pant pant
PLEASE...
AH!
A MAN I'VE NEVER SEEN BEFORE IS RUNNING FOR HIS LIFE.

PLEASE...
STOP...
HELP ME.
DON'T--
AHHHHHHH!
RUNNING FROM SOMEONE WITH VILE'S SCREAMS IN HIS HEAD.
HOW CAN I KNOW THIS?
I CAN FEEL IT THREADED THROUGH EVERY NERVE IN MY BODY.
IT'S LIKE I'M UNDERWATER AGAIN, BUT THIS TIME...

...I CAN BREATHE.
OKAY. I HEAR MY VOICE IN MY HEAD.
NOT VILE'S.
WHATEVER THIS IS, HE'S NOT CONTROLLING ME.
THE NURSE SAID THEY CLEARED THE PARASITE.
SO, I CONTROL ME.
MY MIND IS $#@&?% MINE.
SO WHAT THE @#&$ IS THIS?
WHAT DO YOU WANT? PLEASE! I DON'T UNDERSTAND.
IT'S GOTHAM. DARK OUT.
IS THIS HAPPENING NOW?

&#@%, IT'S SO CLOSE.
I CAN TASTE. COPPER.
BLOOD.
GRAVEL UNDER MY FEET.
MY HEART BEATING FAST.
BECAUSE I'M CATCHING UP.

$#&@!
$#&@!
I KNOW IT'S NOT VILE. I REMEMBER STABBING HIM DEEP ENOUGH THAT HE WASN'T RUNNING OFF ANYWHERE AFTERWARD.*
*IT'S TRUE, SHE DID. DTC #1039 AGAIN. --PAUL
THIS IS PROBABLY-- THIS COULD BE NOTHING.
CAUTION
CONSTRUCTION ZONE
UNAUTHORIZED PERSONNEL
KEEP OUT
I MEAN, I WAS JUST INFECTED BY A BLOOD-LUSTING PARASITE.
I SHOULD BE IN BED, OR, AT THE VERY LEAST, NOT GEARING UP.
I'LL GO OUT THERE. PROVE TO MYSELF THAT THIS IS...WHAT? A GHOST.
A MEDICAL HALLUCINATION.
$#&@!
Pant pant
$#@!
THEN I'LL COME BACK HOME AND ORDER A PIZZA. FINE.

OKAY. WHAT DO I SEE? HE'S RUNNING.
THERE ARE OLD TRACKS...
WATER... CONSTRUCTION.

WHERE WOULD THERE BE ALL THOSE THINGS AND NOT ENOUGH PEOPLE AROUND THAT SOMEONE WOULD HAVE CALLED THE COPS?
THE DOCKS.

OKAY, NOW WE'RE AT THE DOCKS. GOOD TIMES.
DANGER
HARD HATS REQUIRED
NOT SEEING ANYONE. GUESS IT WAS A FLASHBA--
PLEASE. STOP! OKAY?
Pant pant
I CAN'T--
SOMEBODY HELP ME!
@&%$.
&$#@! SOMEBODY HELP ME!
STOP!

IT'S REAL.
THWIK
GHAAAA!
AHHHHHH!
STOP HIM! PLEASE! HE'S STILL--

WHAT THE %#$&!
WHAT THE $@#$ IS WRONG WITH YOU?
GRAAAHHHH!
CAN YOU RUN?
I DON'T-- WHAT-- WHAT IS--
GET OUT OF HERE. CALL AN AMBULANCE.
GRAAAHHHH!
FOR ME?

THAK
FOR HIM.
I DON'T KNOW WHEN VILE INFECTED YOU.
GO!
I DON'T KNOW WHY I CAN SEE WHAT YOU SEE.
IS IT POSSIBLE THAT VILE LEFT DEEPER HOOKS IN ME SOMEHOW?
K-- KI--
HE'S GONE.
IS THIS WHAT HAPPENS WHEN YOUR VICTIMS SURVIVE?
CAN YOU HEAR ME, VILE?
"I WANT YOU TO KNOW. IF YOU WERE TRYING TO HOLD ON TO ME..."
BWOOD BWOOD
EMERGENCY

"...THAT WAS A MISTAKE."
Gotham
DRIVE-IN
DOUBLE FEATURE
CLASSIC MOVIES!
Shhhhhhh!
BT860
GOTHAM

DUN DUN DUN DUN
RED ROVER
BRU717

I'M TRYING TO ENJOY THE MOVIE!
YOU'RE YELLING!
THESE MURDEROUS PUPPETS OF YOURS?
I DON'T KNOW HOW OR WHY.
BUT I CAN SEE WHAT THEY SEE NOW.
WHAT THE HELL IS THAT?!
IS HE RUNNING AT US?
SMASH
RUN!
RUN!

ARE MANY BUT I'M $#@!$%& FAST.
YOU THINK YOU'RE THE HUNTER?
&%$#@?&
HUNTRESS.

AND NOW I'M HUNTING YOU.
HOLY &#$@!
JOHN!
CLICK
I'M COMING!
THUD
I'M GOING TO CATCH EACH AND EVERY ONE OF YOUR PARASITE ZOMBIE WHATEVERS.
SAVE THE ONES I CAN.
Gotham
DRIVE-IN
DOUBLE FEATURE
AND IF I CAN'T SAVE THEM...
...I CAN AT LEAST STOP THEM.

I CAN HEAR THEM.
I CAN HEAR THEIR VICTIMS CRYING FOR HELP.
A *CHORUS.*
WITH SHARP POINTS...
...WHERE THE MADNESS CLEARS.

CHAAAAAA!
CHOP
DANIEL! WHAT IS WRONG WITH YOU?! DANIEL, STOP!
DANIEL!
THUNK
DANIEL?

DANIEL? DANIEL?
OH MY GOD.
GET BACK.
CALL AN AMBULANCE.
Pant pant pant
SSSSSSSS...
SSEEEEEEEEE YOOOOOUUU...

VILE?
SEEEEEEE YOU.
CAAAN'T STOP ME.
HAVE YOUUUUUU.
YOU **HAD** ME AND I **GOT AWAY.** I'M NOT LETTING YOU IN AGAIN.

I'M GOING TO STOP THIS.
ALL OF THIS.
DO YOU HEAR ME?
SQUISH

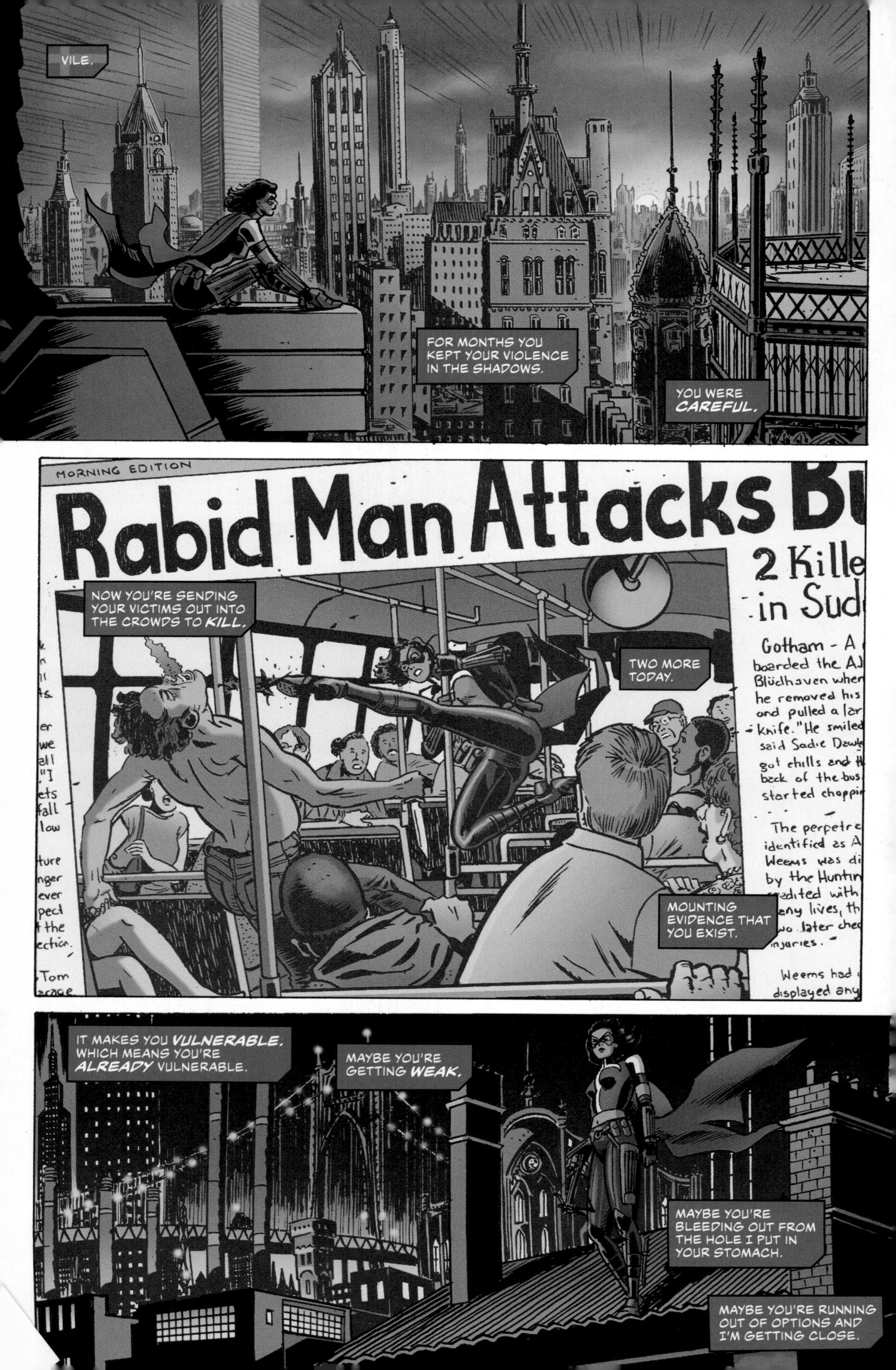

VILE.
FOR MONTHS YOU KEPT YOUR VIOLENCE IN THE SHADOWS.
YOU WERE CAREFUL.
MORNING EDITION
Rabid Man Attacks Bu
2 Kille
in Sud
Gotham - A
boarded the AJ
Blüdhaven when
he removed his
and pulled a lar
knife. "He smiled
said Sadie Dawk
got chills and th
back of the bus
started choppin
The perpetra
identified as A
Weems was di
by the Huntin
credited with
many lives, th
two later chec
injuries.
Weems had
displayed any
NOW YOU'RE SENDING YOUR VICTIMS OUT INTO THE CROWDS TO KILL.
TWO MORE TODAY.
MOUNTING EVIDENCE THAT YOU EXIST.
IT MAKES YOU VULNERABLE. WHICH MEANS YOU'RE ALREADY VULNERABLE.
MAYBE YOU'RE GETTING WEAK.
MAYBE YOU'RE BLEEDING OUT FROM THE HOLE I PUT IN YOUR STOMACH.
MAYBE YOU'RE RUNNING OUT OF OPTIONS AND I'M GETTING CLOSE.

AND MAYBE...
&$@#.
HEY! THERE YOU ARE.
WHERE IS BATMAN?
IN A WAREHOUSE. CHASING WORTH.
WHAT'S GOING ON?
BATMAN.
GOTHAM PLASTIC WO
BATMAN IS INFECTED.
SO MAYBE THIS IS ABOUT TO GET MUCH, MUCH WORSE.

YOU WON'T STOP.
BUT I'M ALSO A CREATURE OF VIOLENCE.
BORN OF VIOLENCE.
AND I WON'T STOP EITHER.
LIFE GOT YOU DOWN? CALL HELPLINE 1800-HELP ME
Follow the Penguin!
TO BE CONTINUED IN DETECTIVE COMICS #1041!

"YOU DIDN'T PROTECT MY DAUGHTER...
WHICH MAKES YOU AS GUILTY AS WAYNE."

DETECTIVE COMICS #1041

cover by DAN MORA

GOTHAM CITY HALL.
AT THE MOMENT, WE DON'T HAVE COMPLETE NUMBERS, MAYOR NAKANO.
THE ONE THING WE KNOW IS THAT THE PARASITE DOES NOT HAVE A LENGTHY GESTATION. SYMPTOMS MANIFEST SOMETIMES WITHIN MINUTES, SOMETIMES WITHIN HOURS.
SYMPTOMS--
THE EFFECT APPEARS TO BE SIMILAR TO RABIES, MAKING THE INFECTED...
"...VIOLENT.
"THE RATE OF INFECTION SO FAR CONFIRMS OUR THEORY THAT THERE IS A LOCAL SOURCE FOR THE INFECTION.
"SOMEONE OR SOMETHING THAT IS INFECTING PEOPLE, WHICH THEN INITIATES A SERIES OF VIOLENT ATTACKS."
"BUT WHAT OR WHO THAT THING IS, WE DON'T KNOW.
WE'VE IDENTIFIED ELEVEN INFECTED BODIES IN THE MORGUE. AND THREE PATIENTS, IN HOSPITAL.
THE GOOD NEWS IS, SO FAR TREATMENT SEEMS TO BE EFFECTIVE.
"OF THE THREE PATIENTS, TWO HAVE RECOVERED, INCLUDING THE REPORTER DEB DONOVAN."
WHO DO I HAVE TO KILL TO GET A WHISKEY SOUR AROUND HERE?
WHAT'S THE PLAN? PRESS CONFERENCE?
GET EVERYONE WE HAVE WORKING ON IT. FIND THE SOURCE. FIND ME SOMETHING TO TELL PEOPLE ABOUT WHAT THEY CAN DO TO AVOID THIS THING.
I'LL DO A PRESS CONFERENCE THIS AFTERNOON.

NOW TELL ME ABOUT THE EXPLOSIONS IN THE SEWER SYSTEM.*
MULTIPLE DETONATOR DEVICES. LOTS OF DAMAGE.
A FEW CRIMINAL ORGANIZATIONS TOOK IT AS AN OPPORTUNITY TO BUST SKULLS AND BREAK WINDOWS.
*SEE DETECTIVE COMICS #1038. --PK
DO WE THINK THIS HAS ANYTHING TO DO WITH THE... PARASITE... THING?
IT'S UNLIKELY ANYONE INFECTED WOULD HAVE THE DEXTERITY TO RIG EXPLOSIVES.
WE'LL NEED CREWS TO DEAL WITH THE INFRA-STRUCTURE SO THE STREETS DON'T CAVE IN.
VILE! GET IN HERE!
ANY MORE WORD ON MR. WORTH SINCE HE LEFT POLICE CUSTODY?
WHICH STILL NEEDS TO BE EXPLAINED TO ME, BY THE WAY...
WE HAVEN'T BEEN ABLE TO--
FIND HIM.
SIR. WE STILL HAVEN'T HEARD FROM VILE. I GUESS HE'S SICK?
CALL HIM. NOW.
WHAT ABOUT BRUCE WAYNE?
"WAYNE WAS RELEASED THIS MORNING.
"THE FIRE AT HIS HOUSE WAS SET LATE LAST NIGHT.
"HE WAS STILL IN THE LOCKUP WHEN IT HAPPENED."

"WAYNE WAS DEFINITELY THE TARGET."
"WHO'S TARGETING HIM?"
WORTH.
WORTH IS A GRIEVING FATHER WHO LOST HIS DAUGHTER, SARAH, TO SENSELESS VIOLENCE.
GOTHAM IS AGELESS
SEWER
AND A MAN OBSESSED WITH HIS OWN "JUSTICE."
ONE NOTE.
HAMMERED OVER AND OVER.
"I WILL NOT STOP."
BUT I NEED TO STOP HIM.
BEFORE HE BLOWS UP THE REST OF MY OPTIONS.
NOT THAT I HAVE MANY LEFT.

SO MUCH FOR MY SEWER OUTPOST...
I KNEW THESE TUNNELS WERE NEVER GOING TO BE AS REMOTE AS THEY NEEDED TO BE.
WORTH CAUGHT SIGHT OF BATMAN CLOSER TO MY LAB THAN I'D WANTED.
AND CLEARLY HE SENT HIS MEN TO FINISH OFF WHAT HIS EXPLOSIVES DIDN'T TOUCH.
AS SOON AS HIS MEN SET FOOT IN THE PERIMETER, MOST OF THE EQUIPMENT WOULD HAVE AUTO-DESTRUCTED.
WHICH IS *REASSURING,* BUT IT STILL LEAVES ME WITHOUT ANY EQUIPMENT.
BATS.
NICE, POSSIBLY UNINTENTIONAL TOUCH.
KLIK
HEY! WHO'S IN THERE?
$#%&!

HEY, MAN! THESE TUNNELS ARE OFF-LIMITS!
WHAT IS IT, KIDS DOWN HERE?
OKAY. SO GOING FORWARD, THE TUNNELS ARE OUT.
I GUESS I SHOULD BE A LITTLE HAPPY THE CITY IS ACTUALLY DOING WORK ON INFRASTRUCTURE.
IF I'M SETTING UP AGAIN, IT'S GOING TO NEED TO HAVE A FEW MORE LAYERS OF SECURITY.
WHICH IS EXPENSIVE.
NEVER EXPECTED I'D HAVE THAT THOUGHT.
FIGHTING GOTHAM'S RICHEST ISN'T EASY.
WHEN YOU'RE NO LONGER GOTHAM'S RICHEST.
AH!
FAIR.

OKAY. LET'S FIGURE OUT WHAT I DO HAVE TO WORK WITH.
IT'S ME, ORACLE.
ON THE PHONE? OLD-SCHOOL.
WHAT CAN I SAY? IN THE LAST 48 HOURS, MY APARTMENT WAS BLOWN UP AND MY MICRO-CAVE WAS SHREDDED. HOW ARE HUNTRESS AND DONOVAN?
M.I.A. AND RECOVERING IN HOSPITAL. HOW WAS PRISON?
TECHNICALLY IT WAS JAIL. MAYBE A MISTAKE.
BECAUSE SOME-ONE BLEW UP YOUR APARTMENT?
COFFEE
COFFEE
I COULDN'T GET CCTV. BUT I'M ASSUMING THIS IS CONNECTED TO A RUMOR I'M FOLLOWING.
ABOUT WORTH AND WHO HE'S TEAMING UP WITH.
PENGUIN.

THERE'S WORD GOING AROUND ABOUT AN ORGANIZATION, A COORDINATED EFFORT TO KILL BRUCE WAYNE.
SEEMS LIKELY WORTH WOULD TEAM UP TO MAKE THAT HAPPEN.
HOW MANY INVOLVED?
THE CALL WENT PRETTY WIDE.
"AN ARMY OF VILLAINS WITH ONE GOAL--"
"KILL BRUCE WAYNE AND BATMAN."
"CORRECT."
I NEED GEAR--
YOU NEED GEAR?
THERE'S A CONSTRUCTION CREW IN THE SEWERS. I DON'T WANT TO RISK BEING SEEN ACCESSING A MICRO-CAVE IF I DON'T HAVE TO.
YOU HAVE AN OLD STASH BY THE DOCKS. I'LL SEND YOU COORDINATES.
IT'S SECURE?
"MOST LIKELY.
WORM CASTINGS
"WHAT NOW?"

WORTH.
I'VE GOT A LOCATION-- HE'S IN ONE OF HIS WAREHOUSES DOWNTOWN.
AND HE'S EXPECTING ME.

BATMAN,
DELIVER BRUCE WAYNE.
THE JURY
OH HEY! I JUST GOT A VISUAL. SO. YOU HAVE AN INVITATION.
BATMAN. DELIVER BRUCE WAYNE. THE JURY
BATMAN
DELIVER WAYNE!
THE JURY
DELIVER
BRUCE
WAYNE
THE JURY
TO MEET A JURY.

WHERE IS HE?
HE'LL BE HERE, ROLAND.
QUIT DOING THAT.
YOU'D BETTER BE **RIGHT,** PENGUIN.
AS SURE AS A DUCK'S $%&# IS--
FWOOMP
IT'S **BATMAN!**
KRAK
ENOUGH!

SO THIS IS THE JURY?
BATMAN. SO GLAD YOU COULD JOIN US. IN BLUE!
OUR ENDEAVOR TODAY SHOULD INTEREST YOU.
A FEW MEMBERS OF THE PARTY CRASHERS, PENGUIN'S MEN, WORTH, THE FALCONES...
WE SEEK JUSTICE.
IN THE MATTER OF THE MURDER OF SARAH WORTH, WHOSE LIFE WAS TAKEN FIVE DAYS AGO BY BRUCE WAYNE.
SARAH WORTH WAS KILLED BY A MAN NAMED NEIL BETTERMAN, WHO WAS--
I OBJECT!

WHERE IS YOUR EVIDENCE?
THE JURY FINDS THAT THE CASE HAS BEEN SULLIED BY THE UNDUE INFLUENCE OF BATMAN AND THE AGENDA OF THE VIGILANTE FORCES HE REPRESENTS.
YOUR TESTIMONY IS TAINTED BY YOUR TIED INTERESTS WITH BRUCE WAYNE.
WHY ARE YOU PROTECTING BRUCE WAYNE?
A SOLID QUESTION.
I PROTECT GOTHAM.
YOU DIDN'T PROTECT MY DAUGHTER.
NO. I DIDN'T.
WHICH MAKES YOU AS GUILTY AS WAYNE.

WHAT IS GOTHAM IF NOT A CITY OF GUILTY MEN?
POWERFUL MEN...
...WHO FAIL TO PROTECT ITS MOST VULNERABLE?
A CITY OF MEN BLINDED BY INJUSTICE, DOOMED TO REPEAT THE CRIMES AGAINST THEM.
BLIND?!
YOU SAY YOU'RE SEEKING JUSTICE.
I SAY YOU SEEK REVENGE.
POLICE INVESTIGATED WAYNE. HIS DNA WAS FOUND IN HER APARTMENT.
HE WAS SEEN WITH HER BY A WOMAN WHO WAS LATER FOUND DEAD. ANOTHER VICTIM OF HIS MADNESS.
WE THE JURY FIND WORTH'S CASE VERY COMPELLING.
A POPULAR OPINION IN A ROOM FULL OF CRIMINALS.
POLICE INVESTIGATED AND CLEARED WAYNE.
AND YET TODAY WE ARE YOUR JUDGE AND JURY.
ENOUGH OF THIS WITTY COURTROOM DRAMA.
FIRE!

MY FATHER ONCE SAID THAT THE REAL MONSTERS OF THIS WORLD ARE MEN WITHOUT REASON.
WHOOM
PING
PING
PING
MEN WHO ONLY KNOW ONE TRUTH.
BRAKKA BRAKKA
BRAKKA BRAKKA
MEN WHO SEE ONLY ONE ANSWER.

BUDDABUDDABUDDABUDDA
MY FATHER WAS WRONG ABOUT FEW THINGS...
...BUT THIS WAS ONE OF THEM.

MEN WITHOUT REASON ARE STILL DANGEROUS, SURE...
KEEP HIM STILL!
HOURS EARLIER.
HUE VILE'S CONTAINMENT CELL.
BUT THEY ARE JUST THE TIP OF THE ICEBERG...
GHAA!
...WHERE MONSTERS ARE CONCERNED.
I SAID KEEP HIM STILL!
SQTCH

NOW.
IN GOTHAM, THE WORLD OF MONSTERS IS VAST.
ZIPP
WHAT--
EVER EXPANDING.

WHAT HAVE YOU DONE?
KRASH
GUHH!
GAAHH!
"ORACLE? ORACLE!"

HUNTRESS! THERE YOU ARE.
I WAS JUST ABOUT TO--
WHERE IS BATMAN?
IN A WARE-HOUSE. CHASING WORTH. WHAT'S GOING ON?
HE'S INFECTED.
HOW DO YOU KNOW?
I CAN'T EXPLAIN IT. I SEE IT. I SEE HIM.*
*HEY, WE'VE SEEN THIS BEFORE! CHECK OUT BATMAN SECRET FILES: HUNTRESS #1, ON SALE NOW, TO FIND OUT WHAT LED HUNTRESS TO THIS MOMENT! --ENCYCLOPEDIA PAUL

"VILE HAS BATMAN."
THE TRUE TERROR OF THIS WORLD IS THE ENDLESS POSSIBILITIES...
...THE MONSTERS YET TO BE BORN.
YESSSSSSSS.
THE JURY PART 1
MARIKO TAMAKI Writer DAN MORA Artist
JORDIE BELLAIRE Colors ADITYA BIDIKAR Letters
DAN MORA Cover LEE BERMEJO Variant Cover
DAVE WIELGOSZ Associate Editor
PAUL KAMINSKI Editor BEN ABERNATHY Group Editor
BATMAN created by BOB KANE with BILL FINGER
NEXT: RAGE OF THE BAT!

"ORACLE TO HUNTRESS! ARE YOU THERE?
WHAT'S HAPPENING?"

DETECTIVE COMICS #1042

cover by DAN MORA

DOWNTOWN GOTHAM CITY.
IN THESE LAST MOMENTS...
...MY FINAL THOUGHTS...
YESSSSSS...
HOW OFTEN DO YOU GET A CHANCE TO KILL BATMAN?
LET'S PUT A HOLE IN HIS HEAD.
THAT'S NOT THE $%*@#& PLAN.
WE NEED TO GET HIM IN A VAN AND TAKE HIM TO MIDTOWN...
...THEN WE WAKE UP VILE.
...SO THEY CAN PUT ON A SHOW.
...AS SOMETHING WITH SHARP EDGES REACHES ACROSS MY BRAIN.

HOW WILL WE KNOW IF THE BAT HAS THE PARASITE, COBBLEPOT?
IT'S NOT AN EXACT SCIENCE, WORTH.
BUT WE SHOULD SEE THE MADNESS SOON.
WE MIGHT NEED TO GIVE VILE A SHOCK FOR SOME REAL RESULTS.
THE CREATURE'S SPINE SLIDES ACROSS MY CONSCIOUSNESS.
NNNGG...
A NEW MIND, A NEW HUNGER...
HIS.
I CAN S-SEE IT.
I REACH FOR SOME HOLD.
FOR SOME PART OF ME TO STAY...
MMMFF...
I CAN'T... HOLD ON...
"YOU BROUGHT HIM TO ME."

HOLY &#@%, HE'S AWAKE? I THOUGHT YOU WERE IN A COMA.
THE BAT IS MINE, NOW.
AAAAHH!
CHOMP
WHAT THE $#@&?!
THE BOSS WANTS TO KNOW WHA--
WHAT THE @#&$ IS GOING ON IN HERE?
THIS &%*#@ GUY IS AWAKE! HE JUST KILLED MAX!

A RABID BATMAN IN THE CENTER OF GOTHAM?
WILL BE QUITE THE STORY ONCE WE GET HIM--
RAGE.
HELP! $%#@! HELP!
WHAT IS--
YESSSSSS.
GRAAAH!
RAGE.
BLAM
BLAM
BLAM
I CAN'T--
--STOP IT.
THE JURY
CONCLUSION
MARIKO TAMAKI Writer
VIKTOR BOGDANOVIC Pencils
DANIEL HENRIQUES & VIKTOR BOGDANOVIC Inks
JORDIE BELLAIRE Colors
ADITYA BIDIKAR Letters
DAN MORA Cover
LEE BERMEJO Variant Cover
DAVE WIELGOSZ Associate Editor
PAUL KAMINSKI Editor
BEN ABERNATHY Group Editor
BATMAN created by BOB KANE with BILL FINGER

WHAT HAPPENED?! MY GUYS ARE GETTING THRASHED!
THE PARASITE TOOK HOLD TOO QUICKLY!
WE NEED TO VACATE IMMEDIATELY.
TATATATATAT
NOT UNTIL I GET WHAT YOU PROMISED ME.
NOW, NOW. NO NEED FOR THAT.
K-ZZAAAK
THIS IS AN UNFORTUNATE RESULT FOR SURE.
GRAAAHH!
BUT NOW I MUST TAKE MY LEAVE, MR. WORTH.
THIS LITTLE VENDETTA OF YOURS AGAINST WAYNE AND THE BAT WILL HAVE TO WAIT FOR ANOTHER DAY.
MMMPH.

FIND HIM.
MY PUPPET.
MY CREATURE.
FIND HIM.
YESSSSSS, HIM.

THAT BIRD %#@#$%!
WOOORTH.
WHAT IS--? WHAT ARE YOU?
NO.
YOU THINK YOU CAN TOUCH ME WITH THIS SICKNESS?
KRRSSH
END HIM NOW.
IT'S ~HUFF~ NOT HUMAN.
TAKE HIM.

DAMMIT...
PANT
PANT
deet
deet
deet
SOMEONE ANSWER!
HE WILL BE OURS.
STOP RIGHT THERE!
YOU HEAR ME?!
WHATEVER YOU ARE, I AM STILL A MAN TO FEAR!
YESSSSSS.

YOU THINK A MONSTER PUTS ICE IN MY VEINS?
THINK AGAIN, BAT.
WHATEVER THAT POISON MADE YOU.
NO ONE TOUCHES ROLAND WORTH.
KLIK

GRAAH!!
WHOOSH
SWACK
BONES SNAP.
BLOOD.
KRNCH
END HIM NOW.
I WON'T.
YOU WILL.

IT IS MY HUNGER YOU OBEY NOW.
OH GOD, PLEASE--
KILL HIM.
NO.

KILL HIM NOW!
RAAAHH!
NO.
ZIP
KRRSH
AAAAHH!
"ORACLE TO HUNTRESS! ARE YOU THERE?
"WHAT'S HAPPENING?"

CARNAGE.
DO YOU SEE BATMAN?
NOT YET. THERE'S FIFTY GUYS IN HERE. ALL TRYING TO KILL EACH OTHER.
VILE'S VICTIMS OR SOME PENGUIN-WORTH WAR?
COULD BE A LITTLE OF BOTH.
PLAN TO FIND BATMAN?
YEAH... IT'S KIND OF WEIRD.
I CAN SEE VILE'S VICTIMS. EVER SINCE I GOT OUT OF THE HOSPITAL.*
I HAVE THIS CONNECTION TO THEM.
RIGHT NOW THERE'S JUST A LOT TO SEE.
*SEE BATMAN SECRET FILES: HUNTRESS #1. --PAUL
HE'S HERE. I KNOW IT.
DAMMIT. WHERE ARE YOU?
HUNTRESS, WHAT'S GOING ON?

THE HUNTER.
IT MUST BE HER.
KILL HER.
KLIK
NO.
"BATMAN?"

HE IS.
&#@%.
WHAT?
HE'S HERE. BUT SO IS...
...VILE.
YOU. THE GIRL WHO SEES MY PUPPETS.
YOU DIE TODAY.
I DON'T KNOW WHAT OR WHO YOU ARE...

...OR WHAT YOU LEFT BEHIND WHEN YOU INFECTED ME.
BUT I'M *DONE* HUNTING DOWN YOUR NIGHTMARE SPAWN.
THIS ENDS--
KRRSSH
HER END. YES.
NO!

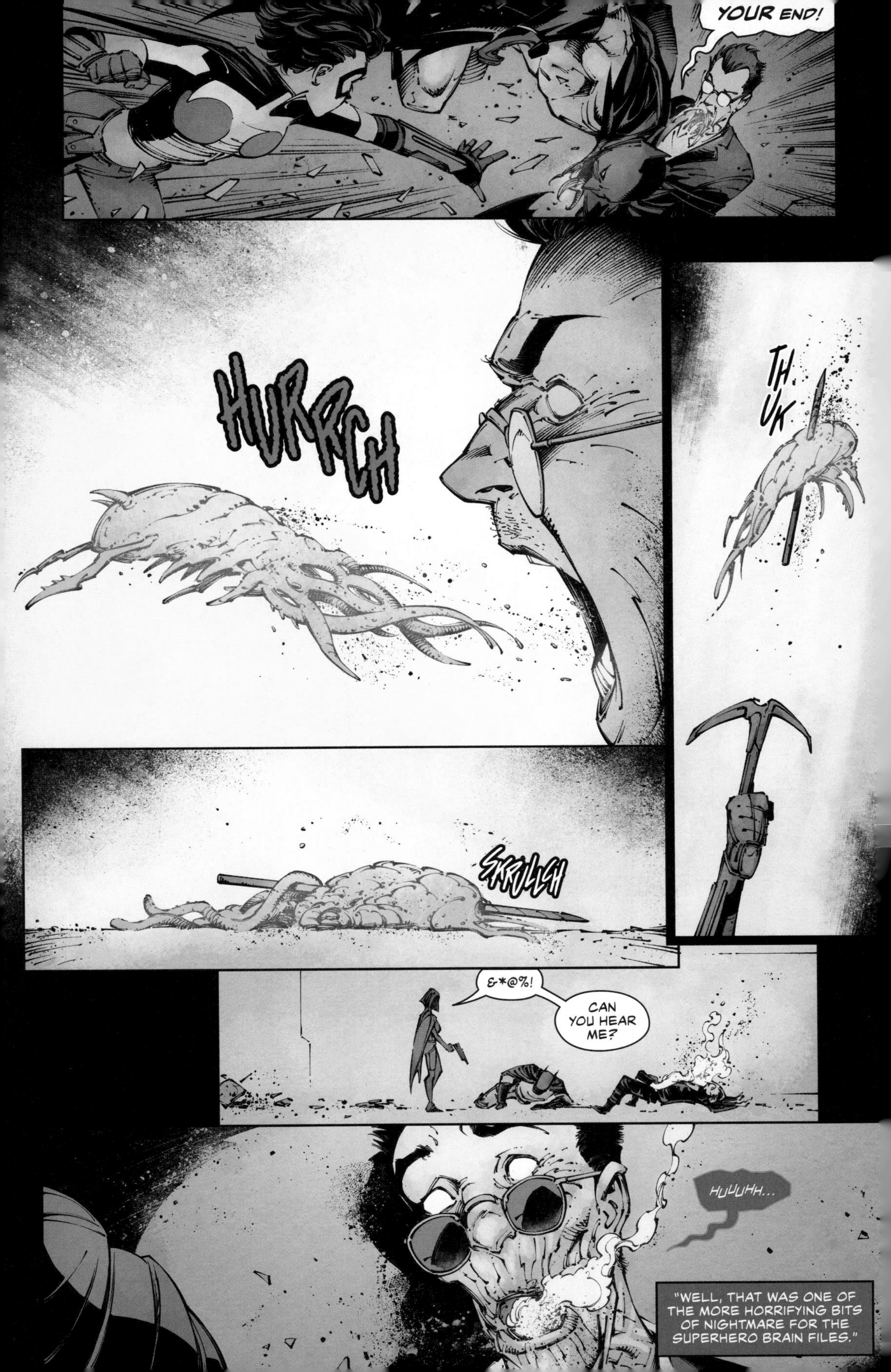
YOUR END!
HURRCH
THUK
SKRUNCH
&*@%!
CAN YOU HEAR ME?
HUUUHH...
"WELL, THAT WAS ONE OF THE MORE HORRIFYING BITS OF NIGHTMARE FOR THE SUPERHERO BRAIN FILES."

I STILL DON'T UNDERSTAND HOW YOU MANAGED TO BOTH NOT KILL WORTH AND TIE YOUR HANDS SO YOU WOULDN'T KILL ANY-ONE ELSE.
TOO MANY NEAR-DEATH EXPERIENCES WHERE MY BRAIN WAS DEPRIVED OF OXYGEN.
I'VE ADAPTED.
I WASN'T EVEN SURE I'D DONE IT UNTIL I SAW HUNTRESS.
Sarah Worth
AND WHATEVER HAD TAKEN CONTROL OF VILE LYING ON THE FLOOR OF THE WAREHOUSE.
HUE VILE DIED IN HOSPITAL SEVEN HOURS LATER.
I CAN'T BELIEVE THEY DARTED YOU WITH VILE SERUM.
NOT A GREAT PLAN. IT MIGHT HAVE ALSO DILUTED THE EFFECT. OR DELAYED ITS FULL POTENCY.
NOW THAT VILE IS DEAD, CAN YOU STILL...SEE? WHAT YOU SAW? THE VISIONS OF HIS VICTIMS?
I GET FLASHES.
THEY'RE NOT AS STRONG. IT'S LIKE SOMEONE ELSE'S DÉJÀ VU.
WHO ARE THE OTHER FLOWERS FOR?
A FRIEND.
YOU KNOW WHERE TO FIND ME, HELENA.
YEAH, YOU TOO.
"YEAH, IT'S ON THE NEWS. WORTH IS NOT DEAD. HOW ABOUT THAT?"

YEAH, A FOUR-STORY DROP AND THE BIG BAG OF HUMAN MONEY LIVED.
ONLY IN GOTHAM.
NAH, IT'D BE A BETTER STORY IF IT WAS SOME-ONE COOL.
BUT I CAN WRITE EIGHT HUNDRED WORDS ABOUT IT.
MISS DONOVAN.
♫
THE GOOD STUFF.
WELL, HOW NEIGHBORLY.
"THANK YOU VERY MUCH, MR. WAYNE."
"UGH."

TELL ME A MORE DISGUSTING JOB THAN CORONER IN GOTHAM.
GROW UP.
MY COUSIN WORKS IN CENTER-VILLE. *TOTALLY* DIFFERENT JOB. LIKE, IMAGINE IT'S *JUST* OLD PEOPLE.
OKAY, *ONE,* THIS GUY'S BRAIN IS SWISS CHEESE. TWO, WHAT ARE THESE? IT'S LIKE... ROE.
EGGS?
JOHN. QUIT IT!
WHAT DO WE DO, REPORT IT?
GAH, THEY'RE EVERY-WHERE! THIS GUY IS FULL OF *EGGS!* $#@%, THAT'S *GROSS.*
ARE THE EGGS... MOVING?
GOD, I HATE THIS JOB!
NEXT: FEAR STATE!

"I DON'T KNOW HOW DEEP THIS GOES."

DANMORA '21

DETECTIVE COMICS #1043

cover by DAN MORA

...YOU WANT TO HEAR SOMETHING GROSS?
I REALLY DON'T.
YOU KNOW ABOUT OPHIO-- OPHIOCORDYCEPS FUNGUS?
NO.
OKAY. SO...
GOTHAM CITY.
CITY SANITATION
AN ANT. STEPS IN A BIT OF FUNGUS JUNK?
RIGHT? LIKE STEPPING IN GUM? EXCEPT THE JUNK GETS INSIDE HIS ANT SKIN.
EXOSKELETON.
RIGHT. SO, THE FUNGUS? STARTS EATING THE ANT FROM THE INSIDE. EATS HIM TILL IT MAKES UP HALF HIS BODY.
THEN IT SENDS OUT LITTLE NEEDLES OF ITSELF INTO THE ANT'S BRAIN. IT WORKS THAT *&$%@# ANT LIKE A PUPPET.
MAKES HIM CRAWL ALL THE WAY UP TO THE SUN. THEN HE FRICKING BITES DOWN ON THE LEAF HE'S STANDING ON AND DIES.
THEN, SO HE'S DEAD, THE FUNGUS GROWS A *&$%&*@ SHOOT OUT OF HIS HEAD AND POOF--
--MORE FUNGUS.
THUMP

WHAT THE &@%$?
THIS HAPPENED TO YOUR AUNT?
*&@%$# ANTS! BUGS! IT'S A BUG FUNGUS!
WHAT THE *&@% KIND OF STORY IS THAT?
PIZZA 24h
MAGISTRATE SANITATION SERVICES
HARLEY WUZ HERE
TELL A GUY A STORY LIKE THAT...
...THIS LATE?
WHATEVER.
MAN, IS IT ME OR IS THE MAGISTRATE EVERYWHERE?
DUDE, WE WORK FOR THE MAGISTRATE.
NOT LIKE THESE GUYS. TALK ABOUT ANTS.
MAGISTRATE SANITATION SERVICES
MAN. JUST SHUT UP AND LET ME DRIVE.
"THIS DECISION ISN'T ABOUT ME."

GOTHAM CITY HALL.
MR. MAYOR, THE MAGISTRATE IS THE ONLY ROAD TO SAFETY FOR THIS CITY. WE AGREED TO ACT SWIFTLY AND SUCCINCTLY.
MY STAFF HAS CONCERNS.
I'M AWARE OF YOUR CONCERNS, BUT THEY ARE...A P.R. PROBLEM.
I HAVE CONCERNS ABOUT WHAT IT MEANS TO TURN GOTHAM'S POLICING AND SECURITY OVER TO A PRIVATE COMPANY. ESPECIALLY A COMPANY THAT HAS ALREADY DISPLAYED SOME... MISSTEPS.
THERE IS A LEGITIMATE POINT ABOUT THE SYSTEMS IN PLACE THAT NEED TO BE PART OF THE FINAL VISION.
THIS IS STILL A CIVIC OFFICE.
MY VISION-- OUR VISION--
MR. SAINT, REGARDLESS OF YOUR NARRATIVE, MY OFFICE HAS WORKED VERY HARD TO MAKE THIS CITY A BETTER PLACE--

TRIED AND FAILED.
WHERE THE MAGISTRATE WILL NOT FAIL.
IT'S THE RESPONSIBILITY OF A POLITICIAN, NOT A "VISIONARY," TO WORRY ABOUT WHAT HAPPENS IF A PLAN DOES FAIL.
THIS CITY WON'T HAVE A FUTURE IF WE DON'T ACT NOW.
THESE ACTIONS HAVE CONSEQUENCES, AND I WILL WEIGH THOSE AS WE MOVE FORWARD.
OKAY. EVERYONE GO HOME. LET'S GET BACK AT THIS AT SEVEN A.M.
THE MAGISTRATE WILL PRESENT US WITH ITS TALKING POINTS AND WE WILL MAKE A STATEMENT.
WHY WON'T NAKANO USE MAGISTRATE SECURITY INSIDE CITY HALL?
THAT'S CURRENTLY THE LEAST OF MY WORRIES.
MR. MAYOR?
WHATEVER SPEECHES NAKANO MAKES OR DOESN'T MAKE, THE MAGISTRATE DOES AND WILL CONTINUE TO RUN THIS CITY.

"THE MAGISTRATE IS THE FUTURE, WHETHER NAKANO LIKES IT OR NOT."
"I KNOW. I'LL BE HOME SOON."
SECURITY
CHRIS. IT'S ALMOST MIDNIGHT.
YOU'RE PUTTING THIS ALL ON YOU.
IT IS ON ME.
YOU ARE ONLY ONE MAN.
...I'LL SEE YOU SOON.
MR. MAYOR.
YES.
MY NAME IS NERO XIX.
FEAR STATE:
NAKANO'S NIGHTMARE Part 1
MARIKO TAMAKI Writer DAN MORA Artist
JORDIE BELLAIRE Colors ADITYA BIDIKAR Letters DAN MORA Cover
LEE BERMEJO, KAEL NGU Variant Covers
DAVE WIELGOSZ Associate Editor PAUL KAMINSKI Editor
BEN ABERNATHY Group Editor
BATMAN created by BOB KANE with BILL FINGER
EDITOR'S NOTE: THIS STORY TAKES PLACE ALONGSIDE BATMAN #113 - ON SALE NOW

I AM A KING.
SECURITY
BLAM
GUNFIRE.
THIS IS MAGISTRATE SECTOR LEADER 18! WHOEVER IS IN THE MAYOR'S OFFICE!
BLAM
$@#&!
BLAM
BLAM
SECURITY
REPORT! REPORT!

I REPORT TO NO MAN. NO ONE IS GREATER THAN ME.
WHO IS THIS?
ANY MAN WHO CALLS HIMSELF GREATER...
...MUST DIE.
TELL YOUR MEN, NAKANO IS NO MORE.
THMP
PLEASE LET EVERY-ONE ELSE BE OUT OF THE BUILDING.
*&$%!
PING
PING

POP POP POP
THREE MORE SHOTS INSIDE.
WE NEED EYES ON NAKANO NOW!
ALL UNITS! GET IN THERE!
WHAT THE *&@$% IS GOING ON?!
ALL UNITS TO THE MAYOR'S OFFICE! REPEAT! ALL UNITS IN THE DOWNTOWN GOTHAM AREA!
MR. MAYOR! OVER HERE!

BUILDING IS NOT SECURE.
WE ARE RECEIVING FIRE!
WHERE IS NAKANO?!
WHAT IS HAPPENING?! WHO ARE YOU? WHERE IS MY SECURITY?!
YOU'RE COMING WITH US.
LET HIM GO.
NOW.
HEY!

WHO DO YOU WORK FOR?!

HRK!
GUH!
WHAT DO YOU WANT WITH THE MAYOR?
WE HAVE EYES ON NAKANO! ALL UNITS! PURSUE BLACK VEHICLE HEADING WEST ON FOURTH!
SQUEEE
WHAT IS THIS?! WHAT DO YOU WANT?!
WHO ARE YOU?!
WHO WE ARE IS NOT IMPORTANT.

WHAT IS IMPORTANT, NAKANO, IS THAT YOU DIE TODAY.
THE ASSAILANTS HAVE THE MAYOR. CODE RED.
CODE RED. REPEAT, CODE RED.
YOU WILL BE THE FIFTH TO DIE. AND NOT THE LAST.
VIGILANTE BATMAN IS ALSO IN PURSUIT.

THINK YOU'RE TAKING ME WITHOUT A FIGHT?!
GRAH!
HOPE YOU'RE BUCKLED UP, NAKANO!
SKREEE
SUSPECT VEHICLE COLLISION REPORTED AT FIFTH AND MAIN!
KRASH

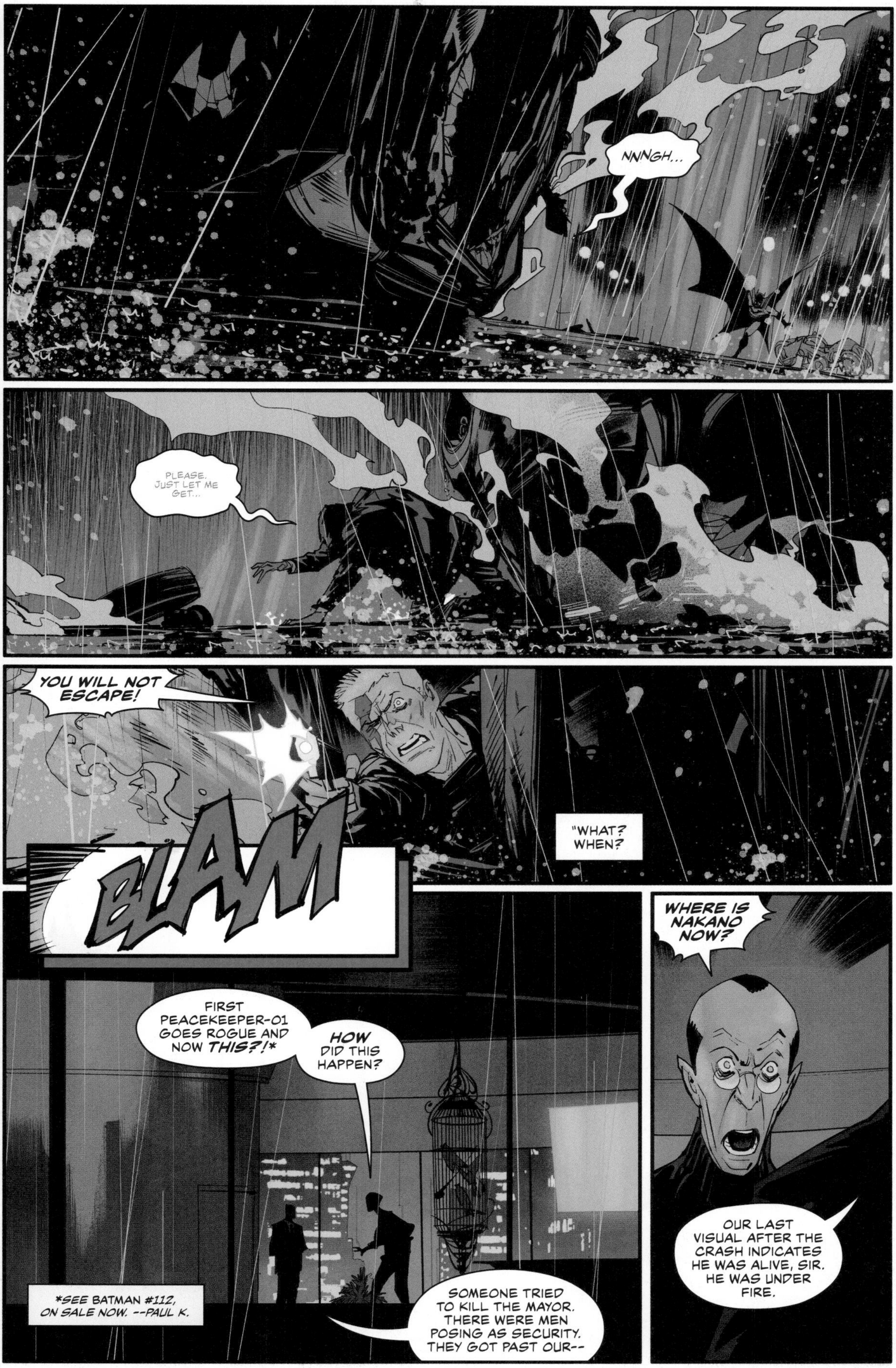
NNNGH...
PLEASE. JUST LET ME GET...
YOU WILL NOT ESCAPE!
"WHAT? WHEN?
BLAM
FIRST PEACEKEEPER-01 GOES ROGUE AND NOW THIS?!*
HOW DID THIS HAPPEN?
*SEE BATMAN #112, ON SALE NOW. --PAUL K.
SOMEONE TRIED TO KILL THE MAYOR. THERE WERE MEN POSING AS SECURITY. THEY GOT PAST OUR--
WHERE IS NAKANO NOW?
OUR LAST VISUAL AFTER THE CRASH INDICATES HE WAS ALIVE, SIR. HE WAS UNDER FIRE.

"TEAMS 54 AND 88 ON SITE SECURING THE AREA AROUND THE GETAWAY VEHICLE. WE BELIEVE NAKANO HAS ESAPED THROUGH THE SEWERS."
"AND BATMAN?"
"BATMAN IS ON SITE..."
I WILL KILL NAKANO! FOR THE KING!
THERE IS NO KING. ONLY JESTERS.
FLK
WSHHH

THE SEWERS ARE FLOODED!
DIVE TEAM IS TWENTY MINUTES FROM LOCATION!
WE HAVE EYES ON BATMAN. HE HAS ENTERED THE SEWERS AFTER NAKANO.

BWHOOOM
SHHHHHH
BRAAAA!
GASP!
WHERE DID HE GO?
NAKANO!

NAKANO!
KOFF
ORACLE? NIGHTWING? BATWOMAN?
I DON'T KNOW IF ANYONE UP THERE CAN HEAR ME. THERE'S BEEN AN ATTACK ON NAKANO.
AT LEAST SEVEN MEN, POSSIBLY MORE. I DON'T KNOW THE STATUS BUT MAGISTRATE IS ON THE SCENE.
KOFF
WHAT THE HELL?
WHAT IS HAPPENING?
DAMMIT.
NAKANO!
THE MAYOR MANAGED TO ESCAPE BUT WE ARE POSSIBLY STILL UNDER ATTACK.
I DO NOT CURRENTLY HAVE A LOCATION ON THE MAYOR. WE SEEM TO HAVE DROPPED INTO SOME SUBLEVEL OF THE UNDER-GROUND SEWER SYSTEM.
HOW MUCH SEWER CAN ONE CITY HAVE?!

I DON'T KNOW HOW DEEP THIS GOES.
OR WHAT'S DOWN THERE.
WHAT THE HELL?
*&@%.
BUT I AM IN PURSUIT.
NEXT: VILE SPAWN!

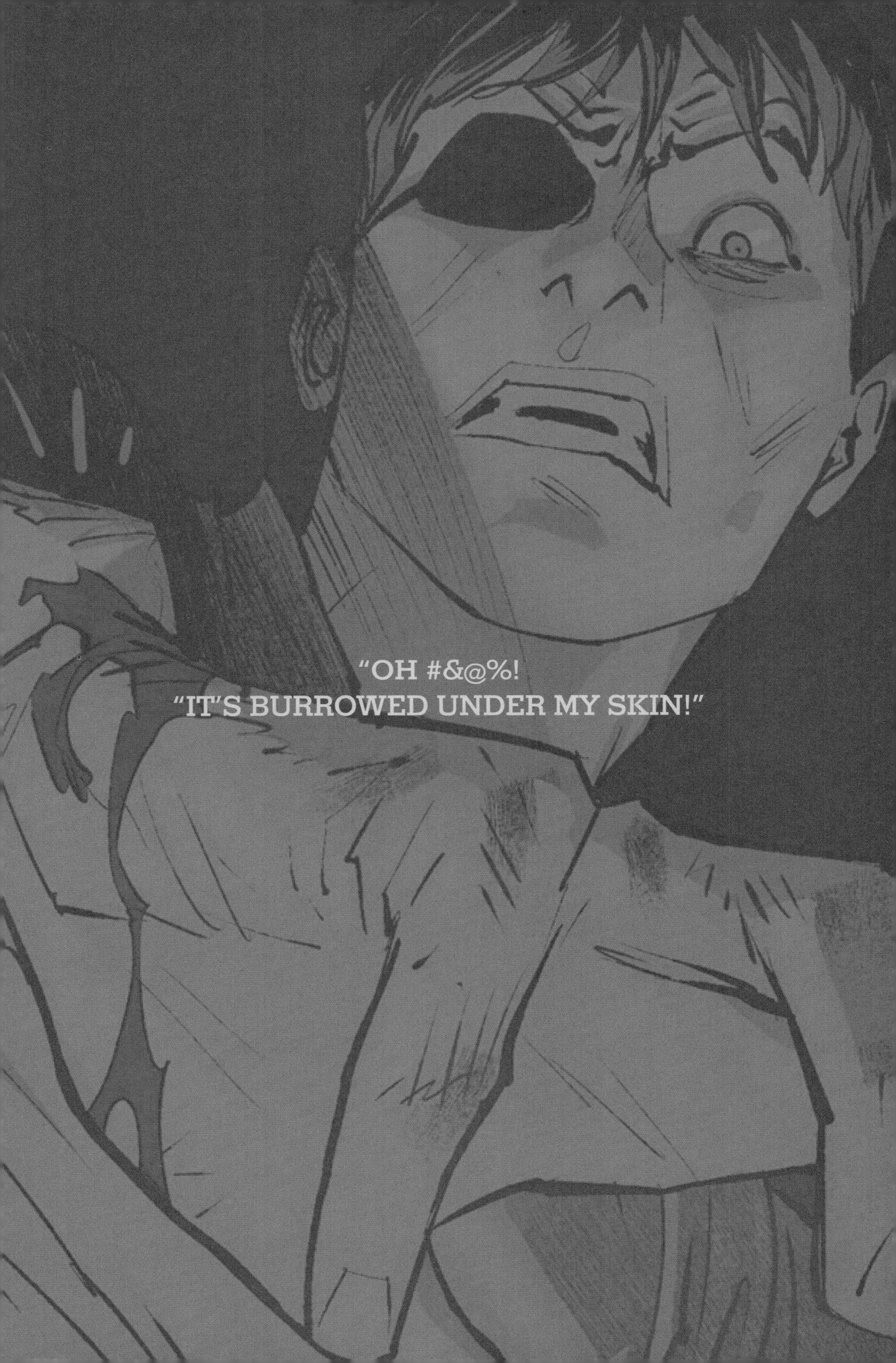
"OH #&@%!
"IT'S BURROWED UNDER MY SKIN!"

DETECTIVE COMICS #1044

cover by DAN MORA

It's a common joke that Gotham City's water is as bad as its politics.
The New Vigilante, a bar on the Upper East Side, sells a drink called the Gotham Tap: whiskey infused with charcoal and a floating black olive. (It's okay.)
SO WHO IS GETTING THESE SANITATION CONTRACTS?
THE CITY IS ON FIRE AND YOU WANT TO TALK ABOUT WATER?
I DO. OFF THE RECORD.
FOR A FUTURE FAVOR?
Maybe it's a strange thing in a time of crisis to want to talk about pipes and morgues.
SURE.
I HEARD IT WAS PENGUIN'S GUYS.
But this is what I'm chasing, for you, humble reader.
CLNK
SEND CRIMINALS TO CLEAN UP THE STREETS, WHO KNOWS WHAT THEY'LL SWEEP UNDER THE RUG.
Because, above-and-beyond current Gotham chaos, our sewers are crumbling, and full of heavy metals and toxins.
OR DOWN THE DRAIN.
No one in Gotham drinks the tap water unless they have to.
Gotham's water is its politics.
Often ignored.
Water is what keeps a city alive.
And while there's no doubt Gotham is alive...
...it's also... rotting.

GOTHAM CITY MORGUE.
DEB DONOVAN IS RIGHT. ABOUT MANY THINGS.
CAUSE OF DEATH-- PARASITIC INFECTION.
GOTHAM IS ROTTEN.
HEY! IS THIS JOHN DOE PART OF THE CITY HALL CASE?
OF COURSE, DECAY IS PART OF THE CYCLE OF EVOLUTION, THE THREAD THAT CONNECTS ORDER AND CHAOS.
WHO OPENED THIS GUY UP? IT'S A MESS IN HERE.
THE SEEDS OF CHANGE IN EVERY TRAGEDY.
FOLLOWING AN ATTEMPT ON HIS LIFE, THE MAN ELECTED TO KEEP GOTHAM ALIVE, MAYOR NAKANO, IS TRAPPED BENEATH ITS STREETS.

I STILL HAVE A LINE OF COMMUNICATION WITH THE SURFACE. BUT IT'S THIN.
ORACLE? CAN YOU HEAR ME?
WHERE ARE YOU, BATMAN?
THE SEWERS CAVED IN. WE'VE DROPPED TO SOME SUB-LEVEL.
I CAN BARELY GET A BEAD ON YOU.
"DO YOU HAVE EYES ON NAKANO?"
"NOT YET."
&%$#!
COME ON, NAKANO. HOW THE &$#% DO YOU GET OUT OF HERE?
WHILE HIS CITY IS IN CHAOS, NAKANO IS TWENTY FEET UNDER.
WITH NO WAY OF REACHING CITY HALL. HIS PEOPLE.

BUT HE'S ALIVE?
I HOPE SO.
WHAT'S THE REPORT ON CITY HALL?
INJURIES, BUT NO CASUALTIES AS OF NOW.
"NO HOSTAGES, FORTUNATELY. THERE'S JUST NERO XIX AND SIX OF HIS MEN.
"THEY'RE MOSTLY HOLED UP IN NAKANO'S OFFICE.
SECURITY
SECURITY
SECURITY
"NO DEMANDS YET, BATMAN."

WE'RE PREPARING TO MOVE — YOU NEED HELP — NAKANO?
KHZZ
I DON'T KNOW — GREAT THIS SIGNAL IS GOING TO BE — ANY DEEPER.
SKHZZ
KHSHZ
--I DON'T WANT ANYONE ELSE PUT AT RISK.
KHZZ
BATMAN? YOU THERE? HELLO?
THESE TUNNELS HAVE BEEN BOMBED MORE THAN ONCE IN THE PAST TWO WEEKS.* EVERYTHING DOWN HERE IS UNSTABLE.
*AS REPEATEDLY SEEN IN THE PAGES OF DETECTIVE COMICS. --CIVIL ENGINEER KAMINSKI
KHZZ
"I'LL TELL YOU — EYES ON NAKANO."
READY TEAMS SIX, SEVEN, AND EIGHT.
READY.
HOLD.
SIR! THERE SEEMS TO BE MOVEMENT ON THE MAIN FLOOR.
WHAT? I TOLD YOU NO ONE GOES IN! WHO IS IT?
I...I THINK THEY CAME FROM THE ROOF? SIR?

GET A VISUAL NOW!
UH. IS THIS THE MAYOR'S OFFICE?
HELLO? UM. I'M LOOKING FOR, UH, MAYOR NAKANO?
WHO ARE YOU?!
M-MAYBE I'M CONFUSED?
THIS IS THE PALACE OF NERO XIX.
YOU WILL PAY FOR YOUR IGNORANCE, WENCH.
OH. I GUESS I MADE A MISTAKE.
OR MAYBE YOU DID.

BUT IT SHOULD BE PRETTY EASY TO RECTIFY.
BATWOMAN!
SOCK
POW
FYI, THERE'S NO REGENCY IN GOTHAM.
YOU WANT THE THRONE, RUN FOR OFFICE.
DEAD END.

ONE CAVE-IN ALREADY. THESE TUNNELS ARE CONCRETE SWISS CHEESE.
NO TELLING WHAT WILL HAPPEN IF I BLAST THROUGH THIS.
BUT NAKANO IS ON THE OTHER SIDE.
NAKANO!
SKITTER SKITTER
GOTHAM'S SEWERS ARE GENERALLY SWIMMING WITH BUGS AND VERMIN.
THIS LOOKS NEW.
BUT ALSO POSSIBLY... FAMILIAR.
SOMETHING IN THE BACK OF MY THROAT TWITCHES AS IT CRAWLS CLOSER.
COULD IT BE CONNECTED TO...
VILE?

VILE?
NAKANO!
WHO IS THAT?
BATMAN...
I'M GOING TO TRY AND GET YOU OUT.
NO.
YOU GET MY MEN IN HERE! YOU GET THE MAGISTRATE! THIS IS A STATE OF EMERGENCY!
THESE TUNNELS ARE UNSOUND. THERE'S BEEN A DOZEN ROUNDS OF EXPLOSIVES IN HERE IN THE LAST MONTH.
WE JUST HAD A CAVE-IN THAT DROPPED US AT LEAST TWENTY FEET.
YOU WANT TO CALL IN AN ARMY TO RISK THEIR LIVES TO FIND YOU IN THE DARK?
WHO WAS THAT AT CITY HALL? WAS THAT YOU AND YOUR... PEOPLE?
THE MAN WHO TRIED TO KILL YOU CALLS HIMSELF NERO XIX. HE AND HIS MEN HAVE TAKEN CITY HALL.
WHAT?
THERE'S NOTHING YOU CAN DO TO HELP FROM DOWN HERE.
THERE'S... SOMETHING HERE. I DON'T KNOW WHAT THEY ARE.
NAKANO.
IF YOU WANT TO GET OUT...

...YOU'RE GOING TO NEED MY HELP.
YOUR HELP. YOU WANT ME TO TRUST YOU? THE MAN WHO KILLED MY PARTNER?
THAT NIGHT AT WAYNE ENTERPRISES.
HIS PARTNER'S MISSTEP AND ONE OF THE JOKER'S TRAPS KILLED HIM, NOT ME.*

MY HELP.
I KNOW THERE'S A PART OF YOU THAT DOESN'T TRUST ME.
BUT YOU'VE ALSO BEEN MAYOR OF GOTHAM LONG ENOUGH TO KNOW BETTER.
YOU'VE SEEN TOO MUCH TO ACT LIKE THERE'S ONLY ONE SIDE TO THAT STORY.
JUST LIKE YOU KNOW THE CLOCK IS TICKING.
AND OUR CHOICES ARE RUNNING OUT.
*SEE DETECTIVE COMICS #1027, WHERE THIS EPIC RUN BEGAN. --PAUL

POP
I--
NAKANO?
SOMETHING'S HAPPENING!
POP
POP
POP
IT'S--
THEY'RE--
VIDEO PHOTO
POP
POP

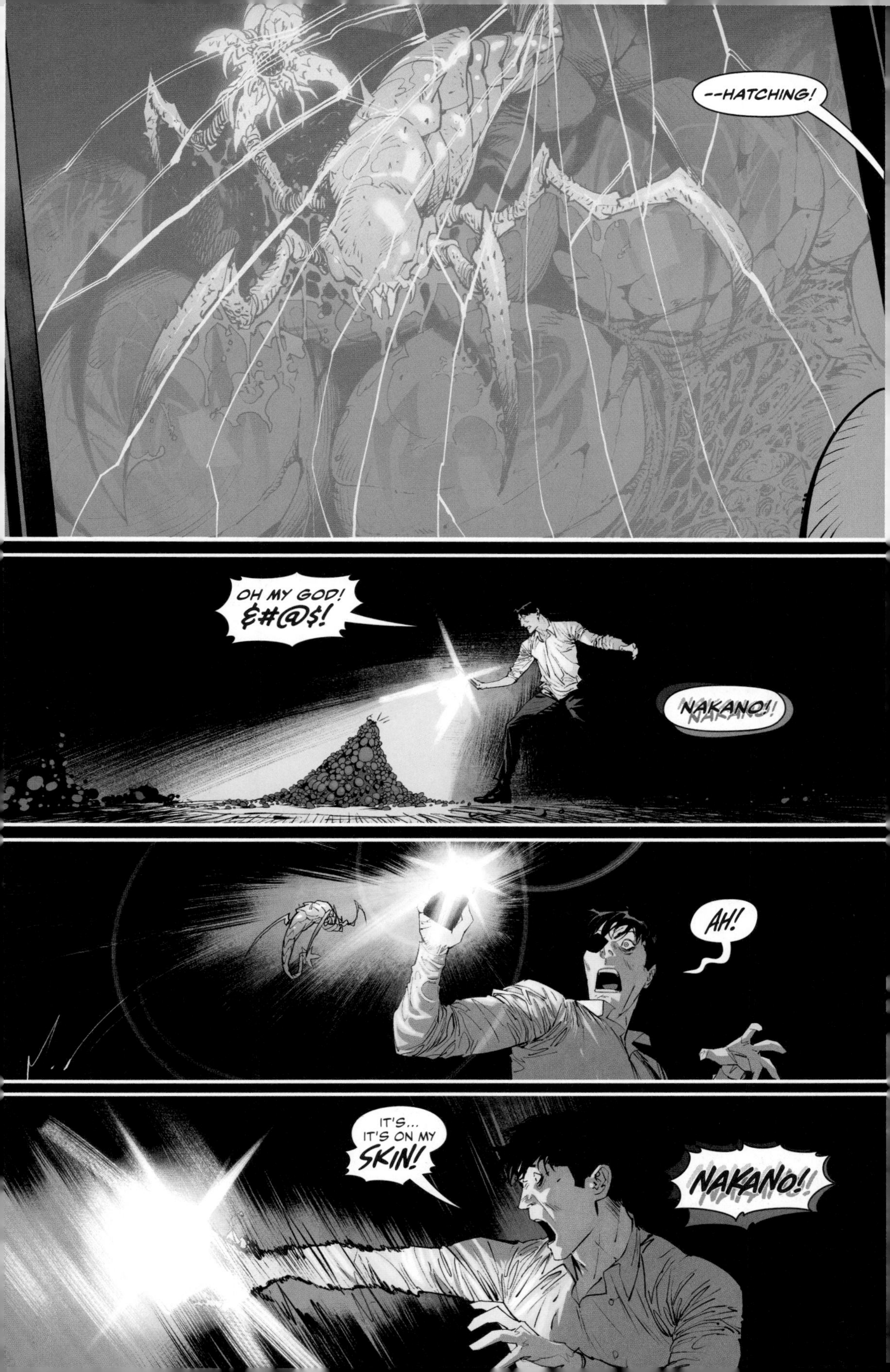
--HATCHING!
OH MY GOD! &#@$!
NAKANO!!
AH!
IT'S... IT'S ON MY SKIN!
NAKANO!!

IF THESE ARE THE SEEDS OF VILE'S MENACE...*
YOU NEED TO GET IT OFF!
NO @&%#!
*BATMAN KNOWS FIRSTHAND WHAT IT'S LIKE TO BE INFECTED WITH THE VIOLENCE PARASITE KNOWN AS VILE, AS SEEN IN DTC #1042! --PAUL
CUT IT OFF!
OH #&@%!
#&@%$!
IT'S BURROWED UNDER MY SKIN!
GET IT OFF NOW!

GAAAH!
KRAK
SPLORCH
THERE'S TOO MANY!
NO CHOICE...
RISK A CAVE-IN OR LET NAKANO BE EATEN ALIVE.
ZHIP
#&%@! HELP ME!
PLEASE!
RUUUMMBLE

&#%$.
OH GOD! GOD, PLEASE!
WATER.
ANOTHER RISK.
POM
PLEASE.
ONE SHOT TO SAVE HIS LIFE.
CHK!

WHICH COULD KILL HIM.
AND ME.
TRUST ME.
PLEASE.
HUMAN BODIES *HAVE* SURVIVED SHOCKS OF MORE THAN TEN AMPS.

THIS WILL BE CONSIDERABLY MORE.
GUUUUUH...
&@$#!

NAKANO? CAN YOU HEAR ME?
COME ON!
WAKE UP!
GET! UP!!

FEAR STATE: NAKANO'S NIGHTMARE Part 2

MARIKO TAMAKI Writer **DAN MORA** Artist
JORDIE BELLAIRE Colors **ADITYA BIDIKAR** Letters
DAN MORA Cover **LEE BERMEJO** Variant Cover
DAVE WIELGOSZ Associate Editor **PAUL KAMINSKI** Editor
BEN ABERNATHY Group Editor
BATMAN created by BOB KANE with BILL FINGER

NEXT: WAKEY WAKEY!

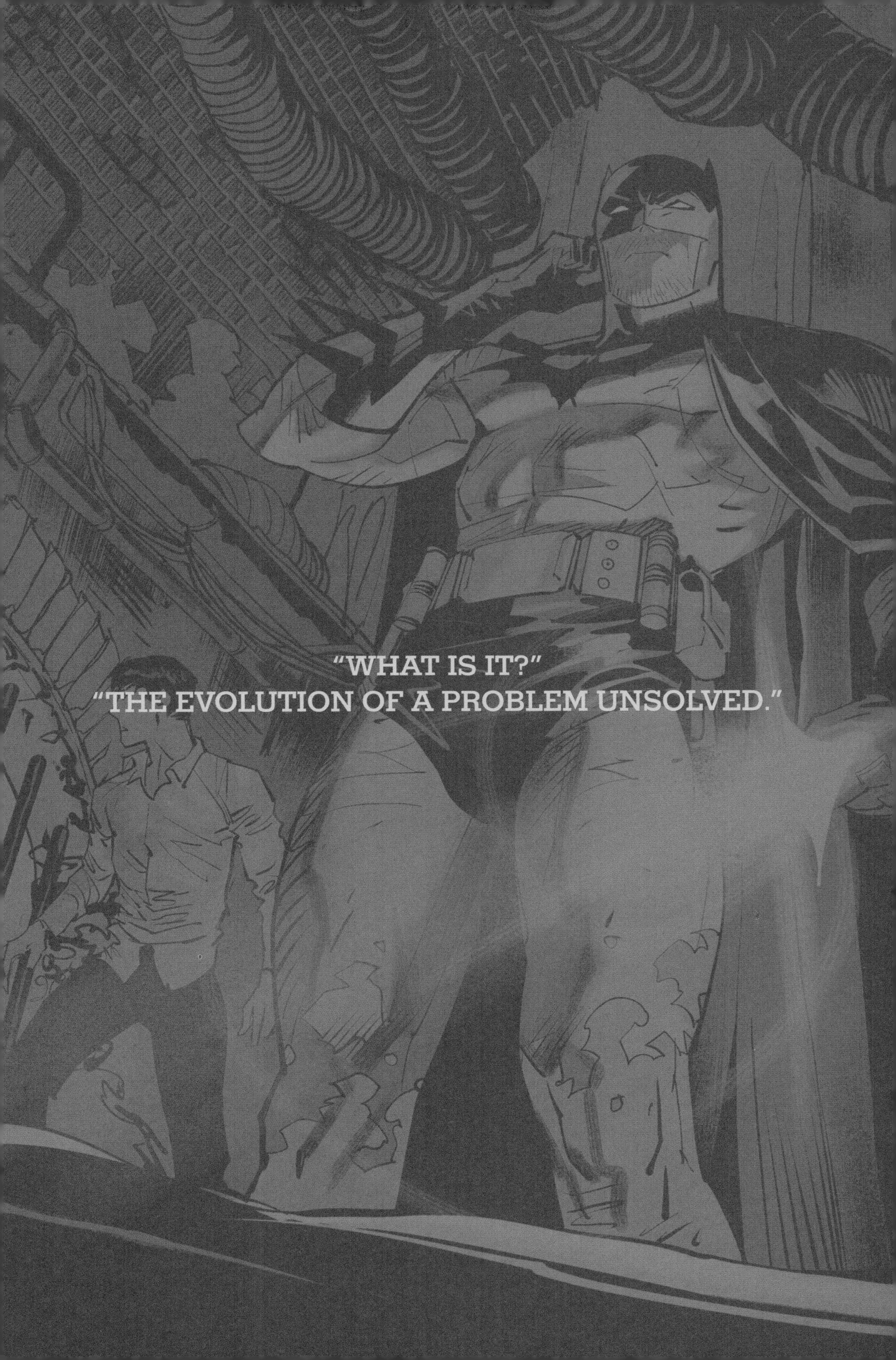
"WHAT IS IT?"
"THE EVOLUTION OF A PROBLEM UNSOLVED."

DETECTIVE COMICS #1045

cover by DAN MORA

GOTHAM CITY...
...NEVER SLEEPS.
WHAT IS IT?
YOU THINK IT'S A BATMAN THING?
LITTLE PARASITE-Y EGGS?
YOU THINK THEY'RE EGGS?
EDITOR'S NOTE: THIS STORY TAKES PLACE ALONGSIDE BATMAN #113, ON SALE NOW!
DEB DONOVAN ONCE WROTE THAT EVERY GOTHAMITE SUFFERS FROM THE KNOWLEDGE THAT EVEN ON ITS QUIETEST NIGHTS, SOMEWHERE IN THE CITY WHERE YOU TRY TO SLEEP...
EW, THEY'RE STICKING TO EACH OTHER.
JOSH! DON'T TOUCH THEM!
...SOME TWISTED CATASTROPHE, SOME GRAND SCHEME, SOME FATAL END, IS ALWAYS BREWING.
THMP
WAKE UP!
EVEN DEB DONOVAN DOESN'T KNOW THE HALF OF IT.
DEF BATMAN STUFF. ALL THE GROSS STUFF IS.
WHAT DOES THAT EVEN MEAN, "BATMAN STUFF"?
TONIGHT GOTHAM'S HARDEST-WORKING CIVIL SERVANT IS DYING FROM A BLAST OF ELECTRICITY THAT I SHOT INTO HIM, TO SAVE HIS LIFE.
WAKE UP!

GHAAAAAAH!
GET THEM OFF ME!
THE PARASITES ARE GONE. I SHOCKED YOU WITH A FEW THOUSAND VOLTS TO KILL THEM.
NOW IT'S A QUESTION OF WHETHER I WAS TOO LATE.
MAYOR NAKANO LIVES.
IF NAKANO IS INFECTED.
OPEN YOUR EYES.
WH-WHAT?
WHAT ARE YOU DOING? GET AWAY FROM ME!
NO ABNORMAL REACTION TO LIGHT.
WHAT DOES THAT MEAN?
IT MEANS YOU'RE NOT INFECTED.
WE NEED TO GET OUT OF HERE.
I FEEL LIKE SOMETHING'S SHREDDED MY INSIDES.
"BATMAN!"

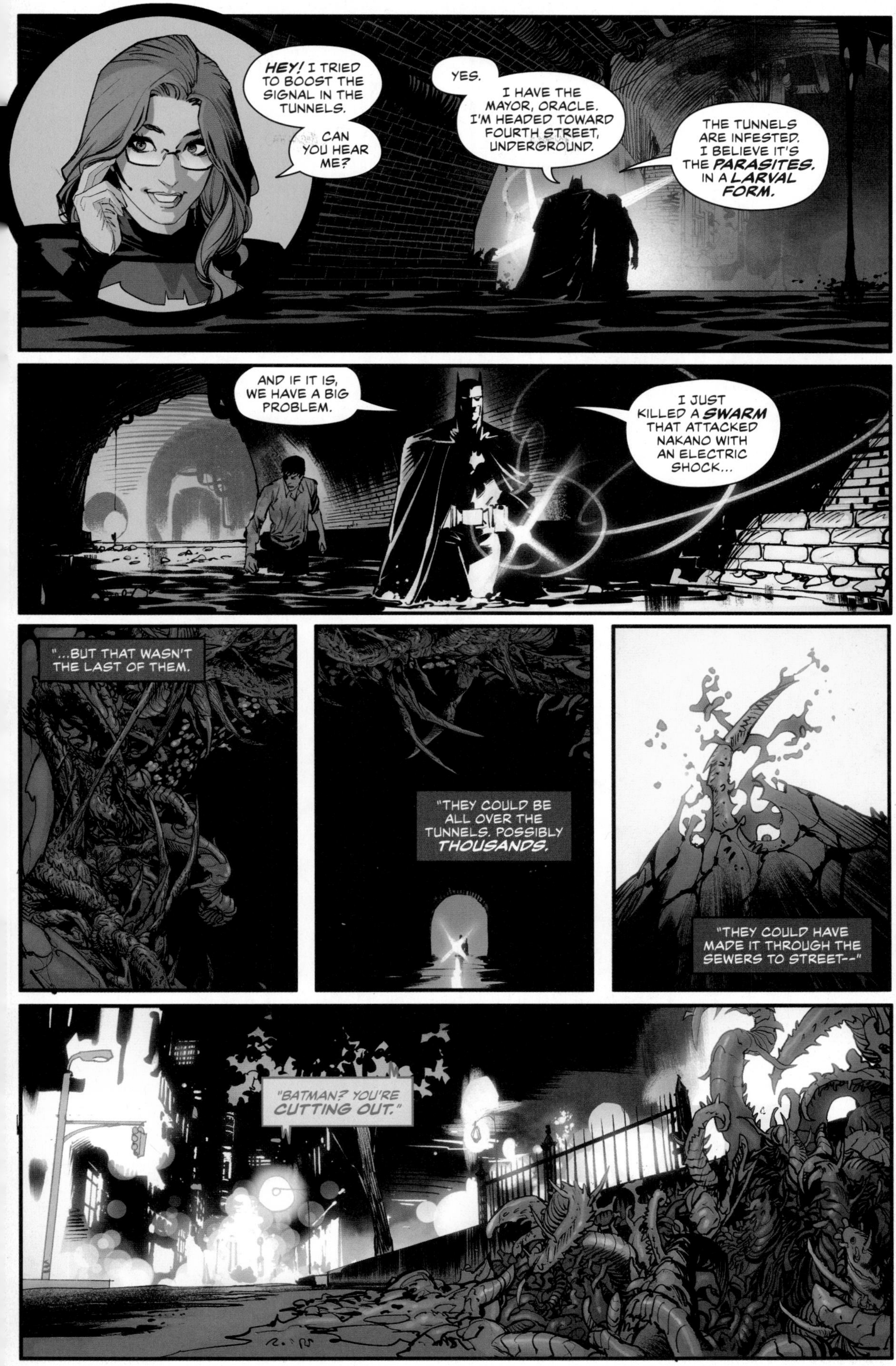
HEY! I TRIED TO BOOST THE SIGNAL IN THE TUNNELS.
CAN YOU HEAR ME?
YES.
I HAVE THE MAYOR, ORACLE. I'M HEADED TOWARD FOURTH STREET, UNDERGROUND.
THE TUNNELS ARE INFESTED. I BELIEVE IT'S THE PARASITES. IN A LARVAL FORM.
AND IF IT IS, WE HAVE A BIG PROBLEM.
I JUST KILLED A SWARM THAT ATTACKED NAKANO WITH AN ELECTRIC SHOCK...
"...BUT THAT WASN'T THE LAST OF THEM.
"THEY COULD BE ALL OVER THE TUNNELS. POSSIBLY THOUSANDS.
"THEY COULD HAVE MADE IT THROUGH THE SEWERS TO STREET--"
"BATMAN? YOU'RE CUTTING OUT."

BATMAN?
@#$%!
OKAY. ORACLE HERE. WE NEED TO GET EYES ON EVERY SEWER ENTRANCE WE CAN. BATMAN WAS HEADED TO FOURTH. LET'S CUT OFF EVERY-THING BELOW TENTH.
THIS IS ORPHAN. I'M DOWNTOWN. ON IT.
WORD IS, A PARASITIC INFECTION COULD BE IN THE CITY SEWER SYSTEM. AND GETTING BIGGER WITH EVERY MINUTE.
THIS IS NIGHTWING. I'M NOT FAR FROM CITY CENTER.
OH, COME ON.
WHAT IS THIS?
SPLORCH

WHAT THE $#$@?!
"ORACLE. I NEED TO GET THE MAYOR TO SAFETY."

ORACLE?
DAMN.
I NEED TO CONTACT MY PEOPLE! I NEED TO SEE WHAT'S--
THE MAN WHO TRIED TO TAKE YOUR OFFICE HOSTAGE, NERO XIX, HAS BEEN TAKEN INTO CUSTODY. THE CITY HALL STAFF ARE ALL SAFE. ONLY MINOR INJURIES.
HEY!
I'M NOT SOME HAPLESS VICTIM HERE. I'M THE MAYOR.
WHATEVER IS HAPPENING, WHATEVER THIS IS, MY TEAM NEEDS TO--
OH MY GOD.

WHAT IS IT?
THE EVOLUTION OF A PROBLEM UNSOLVED.
WHAT--
WHAT--
WE NEED TO GET OUT OF HERE, NOW.

EVOLUTION?
EVOLUTION OF WHAT?
THIS IS AN INFESTATION!
SPREADING FASTER THAN YOUR FORCES WILL BE ABLE TO CONTAIN.
SPLASH!
HEY!

IF YOU KNOW WHAT THIS IS, TELL ME.
I DON'T HAVE A DEFINITIVE ANSWER.
TELL ME.
WHAT.
YOU KNOW.
I STRONGLY SUSPECT WHAT ATTACKED YOU EARLIER IS THE LARVAL STAGE OF THE PARASITE.
PARASITE? IS THIS RELATED TO THE ATTACKS EARLIER THIS MONTH? THE INFECTIONS?
YES.
THERE HAVEN'T BEEN ANY INCIDENTS REPORTED IN WEEKS.
NOT REPORTED DOESN'T MEAN THE PROBLEM WAS SOLVED.
I THINK THE PARASITE HAS SOMEHOW RELEASED EGGS INTO THE SEWERS.
AND POSSIBLY MUTATED IN WHATEVER SLUDGE CITY SANITATION HASN'T CLEANED OUT OF THESE SEWERS IN YEARS.
HOW DO I KNOW THIS ISN'T YOUR PLOT?
BECAUSE HOWEVER YOU THINK I WAS INVOLVED IN YOUR PARTNER'S DEATH...
...I JUST SAVED YOUR LIFE.
THEN WHY DO YOU KNOW SO MUCH ABOUT THIS?
"THREE DAYS AGO I WAS INFECTED.
"BY A SAMPLE INJECTED BY MR. WORTH."
"WORTH?"
"HE AND PENGUIN INFECTED ME WITH A SAMPLE DRAWN FROM THE SOURCE OF THIS INFESTATION..."

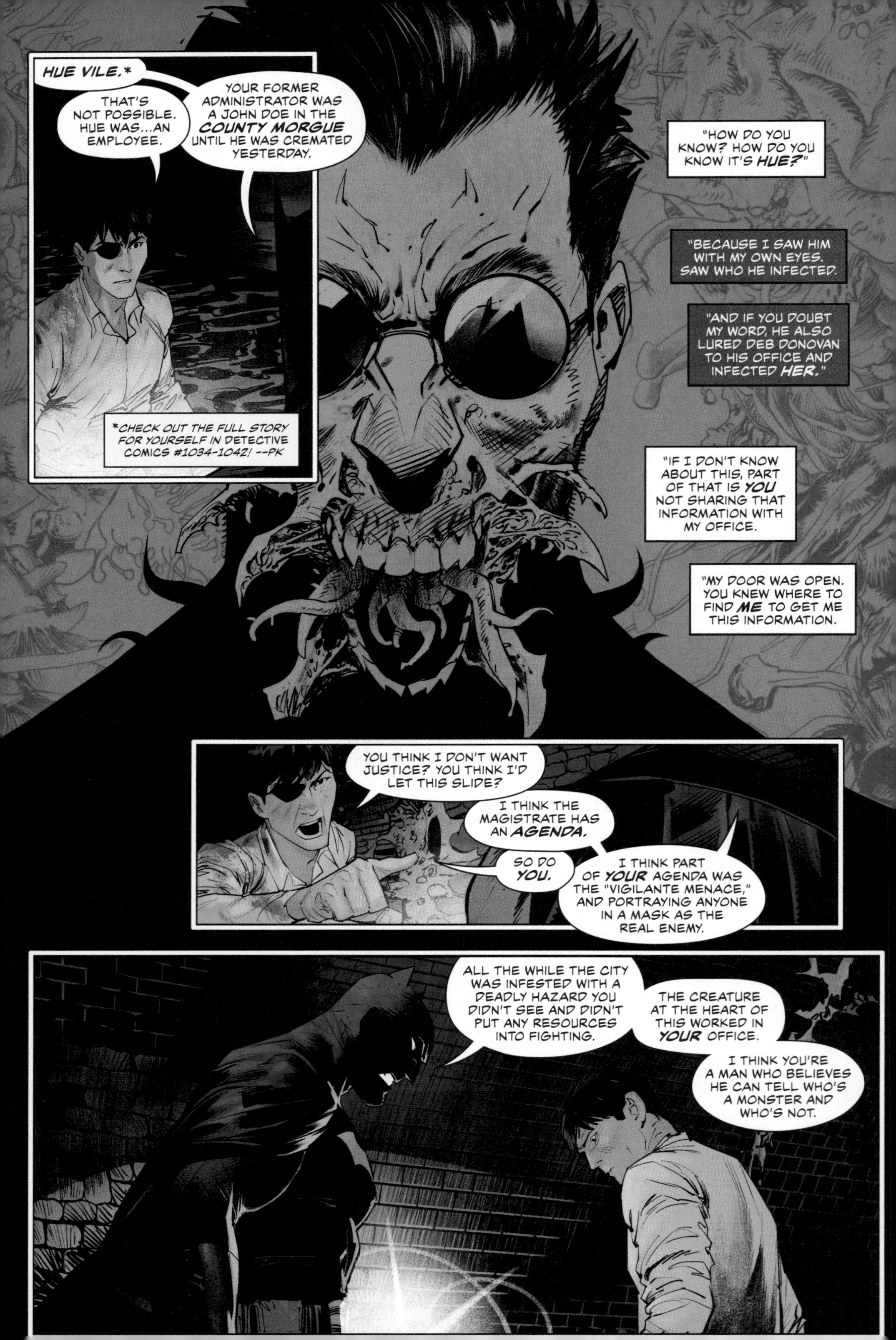
HUE VILE.*
THAT'S NOT POSSIBLE. HUE WAS...AN EMPLOYEE.
YOUR FORMER ADMINISTRATOR WAS A JOHN DOE IN THE COUNTY MORGUE UNTIL HE WAS CREMATED YESTERDAY.
*CHECK OUT THE FULL STORY FOR YOURSELF IN DETECTIVE COMICS #1034-1042! --PK
"HOW DO YOU KNOW? HOW DO YOU KNOW IT'S HUE?"
"BECAUSE I SAW HIM WITH MY OWN EYES. SAW WHO HE INFECTED.
"AND IF YOU DOUBT MY WORD, HE ALSO LURED DEB DONOVAN TO HIS OFFICE AND INFECTED HER."
"IF I DON'T KNOW ABOUT THIS, PART OF THAT IS YOU NOT SHARING THAT INFORMATION WITH MY OFFICE.
"MY DOOR WAS OPEN. YOU KNEW WHERE TO FIND ME TO GET ME THIS INFORMATION.
YOU THINK I DON'T WANT JUSTICE? YOU THINK I'D LET THIS SLIDE?
I THINK THE MAGISTRATE HAS AN AGENDA.
SO DO YOU.
I THINK PART OF YOUR AGENDA WAS THE "VIGILANTE MENACE," AND PORTRAYING ANYONE IN A MASK AS THE REAL ENEMY.
ALL THE WHILE THE CITY WAS INFESTED WITH A DEADLY HAZARD YOU DIDN'T SEE AND DIDN'T PUT ANY RESOURCES INTO FIGHTING.
THE CREATURE AT THE HEART OF THIS WORKED IN YOUR OFFICE.
I THINK YOU'RE A MAN WHO BELIEVES HE CAN TELL WHO'S A MONSTER AND WHO'S NOT.

"I THINK GOTHAM IS A CITY FULL OF MONSTERS *YOU COULDN'T SEE.*"
THIS IS BATWOMAN. AT FORTY-NINTH AND TENTH.
ORACLE. CHANGE OF PLAN.
CUT OFF *EVERYTHING* BELOW TWENTIETH.

BATMAN? THIS IS BATWOMAN. ARE YOU OUT OF THE TUNNELS?
I'M ABOVE GROUND. KEEP THE PERIMETER.
WHAT ARE YOU DOING?
GO THREE BLOCKS NORTH.
GET THE MAGISTRATE TO KEEP GOTHAM'S CITIZENS NORTH OF TWENTIETH.
*&$%.

HELLLP!
RUN!
MR. MAYOR?
GO! GET COVER!
mobile
WHERE ARE YOU GOING? MR. MAYOR! THERE'S A &*$@# GROSS THING!
MONSTERS.
MY GOD.

ZZZZZZZZZZZ
IT'S... IT'S GOING TO KILL HIM.
KLIK
GRRA--
ELECTRICITY.
HE SAID HE SHOCKED ME...
CHK

NAKANO! GET OUT OF HERE!
I'M GOING TO HELP YOU! YOU SHOCKED ME TO KILL THEM, RIGHT?
HEY, THIS IS NIGHTWING. GOT A MAGISTRATE RIDE.
DAMMIT. IT'S NOT ENOUGH.
IT'S TOO BIG.
I'VE GOT A BIO READ. THE ELECTRO-SHOCK IS DOING DAMAGE--I THINK WE JUST NEED TO UP THE AMPS TO FRY THIS THING.
POWERING UP.
FIRING.

FIRING AGAIN!
NAKANO!
UNLESS YOU WANT ANOTHER TEN THOUSAND VOLTS.
LET'S ZAP THIS BUG-SQUID ONE MORE TIME.
THEN I THINK IT'S CALAMARI FOR EVERY-ONE.
SEE! I TOLD YOU!

MAGISTRATE RETURN
ORDER TO DOWNTOWN
Batman spotted on scene
GOOD THING THE MAGISTRATE WAS THERE.
THOSE BUG THINGS! THEY TURNED INTO A FRICKING MONSTER!
COFFEE
I TOLD YOU IT WAS A BATMAN THING.
IF IT WASN'T FOR ME, YOU'D BE UP TO YOUR EYEBALLS IN BUG GUTS RIGHT NOW.
NAKANO SHOWS NO SYMPTOMS. BROKEN RIB. OTHERWISE NOTHING.
IT'S WORTH SHARING THE INFORMATION THAT WHATEVER THEY USED TO TREAT YOU FOR THE PARASITE KEPT YOU FROM GETTING INFECTED AGAIN.
GET IT TO NAKANO'S OFFICE.
HEY, ARE WE COORDINATING WITH THE MAYOR NOW?
WE'RE... WORKING ON IT.

IS THERE A FUTURE BETWEEN THE MAYOR AND THE VIGILANTE WHO WAS ONCE HIS SWORN ENEMY?
TIME WILL TELL.
"MR. MAYOR?"
"YES. REPORT."

THEY'VE ARRESTED THE H.R. PLANT WHO WAS HIRING NERO XIX AND HIS MEN. THE CHIEF HAS A REPORT FOR YOU. I GUESS WE NEED TO GET A NEW H.R. TO HIRE A NEW H.R. MANAGER.
WE HAVE A MEETING WITH THE MAGISTRATE, WHICH HAS BEEN RESCHEDULED TO LATER TODAY.
THE MAGISTRATE HAS TAKEN OVER SECURITY FOR THE BUILDING.
THEY HAVE A REPORT ON THE INCIDENTS OF...YESTERDAY... AND THEY'RE READY TO PRESENT IT. ON NERO XIX AND THE PARASITES.
I HAVE SOME INFORMATION AS WELL THAT I WANT THIS OFFICE TO LOOK INTO.
FROM WHO?
SOMEONE WE'RE COORDINATING WITH. NOW.
AND I WANT TO SEE DEB DONOVAN.
TELL HER I WANT TO TALK ABOUT CITY INFRA-STRUCTURE. ALL OF IT.
TELL HER IT WILL STAY IN THIS OFFICE.
AND I'LL GIVE HER AN EXCLUSIVE INTERVIEW FOR HER TROUBLE.
IN THE MEANTIME, WE'RE GOING TO START MAKING A LIST. A BETTER LIST...
OF WHAT?

MONSTERS.
FEAR STATE:
NAKANO'S NIGHTMARE Finale
MARIKO TAMAKI Writer DAN MORA Artist
JORDIE BELLAIRE Colors ADITYA BIDIKAR Letters
DAN MORA Cover LEE BERMEJO Variant Cover
DAVE WIELGOSZ Associate Editor PAUL KAMINSKI Editor
BEN ABERNATHY Group Editor
BATMAN created by BOB KANE with BILL FINGER
NEXT: The Last Dark Knight in Gotham!

DETECTIVE COMICS BACKUP FEATURES

THERE IS A MAN WAITING IN A GRAVEYARD IN GOTHAM CITY.
A COFFIN HAS JUST BEEN LOWERED. THERE WERE NO MOURNERS AT THE GRAVESIDE.
A PRIEST SAID A FEW SHORT WORDS. STOCK, VAGUE PASSAGES READ FOR A MAN HE'D NEVER MET.
LANGSTROM
THERE WAS A SINGLE WREATH OF FLOWERS PAID FOR, LIKE THE FUNERAL, BY AN ANONYMOUS DONOR.
THERE IS A MAN WAITING IN A GRAVEYARD, JUST IN CASE ANYONE COMES.
IN CASE ANYONE CARES.
the quiet and unsung death of kirk langstrom
DAN WATTERS Writer
MAX RAYNOR Artist
ARIF PRIANTO Colors
ROB LEIGH Letters
DAVE WIELGOSZ Associate Editor
PAUL KAMINSKI Editor
THE DARK KNIGHT WAITS AT THE GRAVE OF KIRK LANGSTROM, HIS HEART HEAVY WITH GUILT.

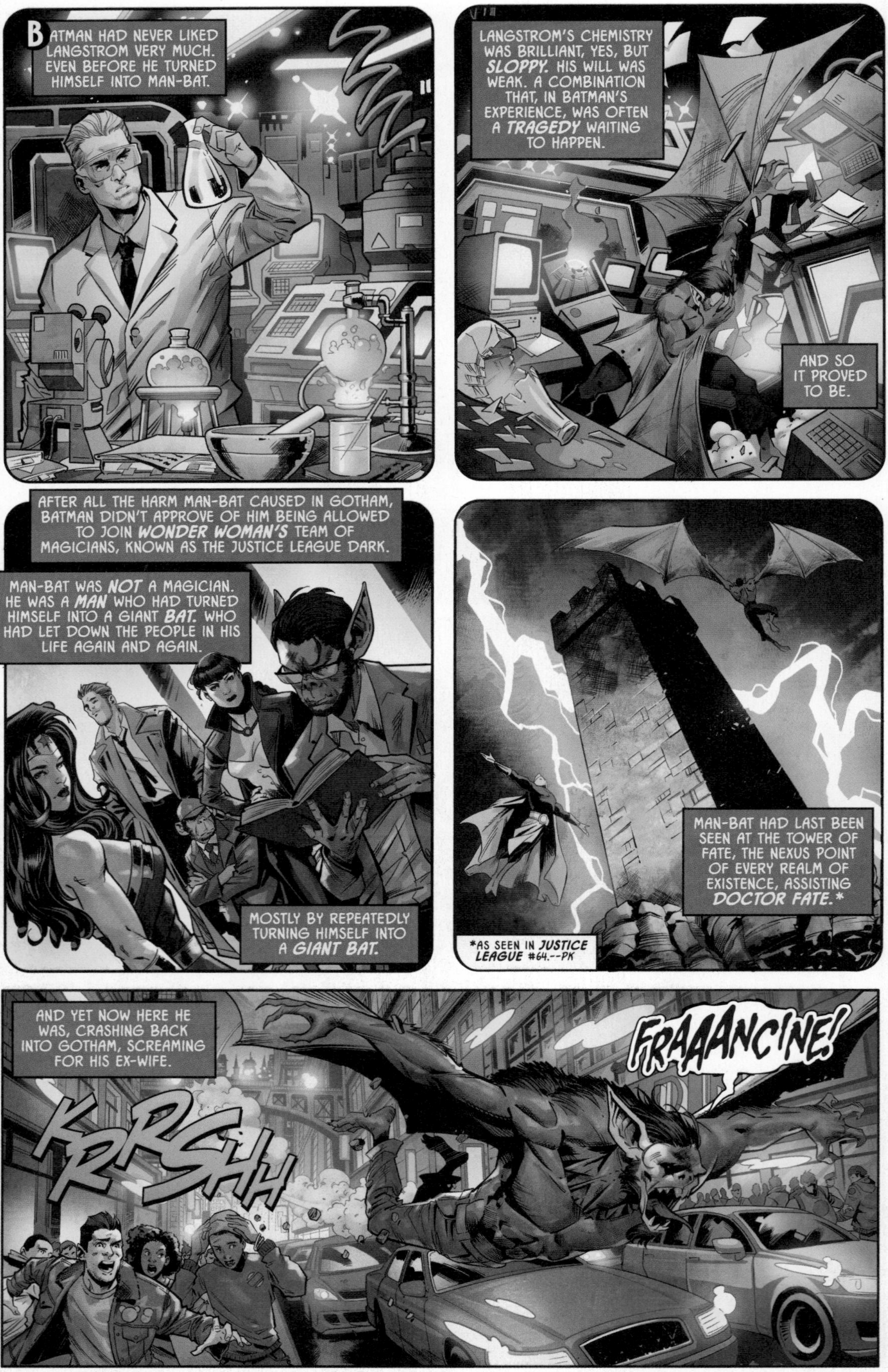
BATMAN HAD NEVER LIKED LANGSTROM VERY MUCH. EVEN BEFORE HE TURNED HIMSELF INTO MAN-BAT.
LANGSTROM'S CHEMISTRY WAS BRILLIANT, YES, BUT SLOPPY. HIS WILL WAS WEAK. A COMBINATION THAT, IN BATMAN'S EXPERIENCE, WAS OFTEN A TRAGEDY WAITING TO HAPPEN.
AND SO IT PROVED TO BE.
AFTER ALL THE HARM MAN-BAT CAUSED IN GOTHAM, BATMAN DIDN'T APPROVE OF HIM BEING ALLOWED TO JOIN WONDER WOMAN'S TEAM OF MAGICIANS, KNOWN AS THE JUSTICE LEAGUE DARK.
MAN-BAT WAS NOT A MAGICIAN. HE WAS A MAN WHO HAD TURNED HIMSELF INTO A GIANT BAT. WHO HAD LET DOWN THE PEOPLE IN HIS LIFE AGAIN AND AGAIN.
MOSTLY BY REPEATEDLY TURNING HIMSELF INTO A GIANT BAT.
MAN-BAT HAD LAST BEEN SEEN AT THE TOWER OF FATE, THE NEXUS POINT OF EVERY REALM OF EXISTENCE, ASSISTING DOCTOR FATE.*
*AS SEEN IN JUSTICE LEAGUE #64.--PK
AND YET NOW HERE HE WAS, CRASHING BACK INTO GOTHAM, SCREAMING FOR HIS EX-WIFE.
FRAAANCINE!
KRRSHH

WAS BATMAN TO BE BLAMED FOR THINKING LANGSTROM HAD REGRESSED?
PUM
FOR THINKING THAT HE WAS GOING TO HURT PEOPLE?
LANGSTROM!
BATMAN! NO, NOT YOU. STAY BACK.
LANGSTROM ALWAYS HURT PEOPLE.
WH-WHERE'S FRANCINE?
I NEED HER. SHE WASN'T AT THE LAB...OR HER HOUSE...
IS THIS WHAT IT WAS ALL ABOUT?
JOIN A TEAM OF HEROES SO YOU COULD PROVE YOURSELF TO HER? TO WIN HER BACK?
NO! YOU DON'T UNDERSTAND.
SHE'S THE ONLY THING... THAT MAKES ME LESS AFRAID.
YOU'VE TAKEN SOMETHING, HAVEN'T YOU? ATTEMPTED TO ADAPT THE MAN-BAT SERUM...
I WAS STABLE, BATMAN. I HAD DONE IT. YOU SAW!*
BUT AT THE TOWER OF FATE, IT SAW ME. IT LOOKED UP FROM SOME HELL...AND THERE I WAS.
WHAT SAW YOU, LANGSTROM?
*SEE MAN-BAT #5. --PK

He CANNOT See Me, FOR i aM WITHIN You.
...WHAT ARE YOU TALKING ABOUT?
oH, HOW He DISDAINS You.
BUT He KNOWS YOU FOR WHAT You aRe, JUST aS i Do.
a WeaK THING.
aN aDDICT.
NO...
a TeRRIFIeD BeaST.

See How He Looks aT You. He KNOWS You're No MoRe THAN THE aNiMaL You aPPeaR To Be.
He KNOWS YouR eVeRY aCT To Be CaRNaL aND SeLF-SeRViNG.
He SeeS You. aND THaT'S WHaT You FeaR.
BATMAN... PLEASE.
IT SHOWED ME! SHOWED ME WHAT IT CAN DO! TH-THE FIRST TIME IT CAME TO EARTH, A WHOLE VILLAGE HAD TO SACRIFICE THEMSELVES TO CONTAIN IT.
IT NEEDS FEAR. FEAR LETS IT THROUGH.
LANGSTROM?!
I-I CAN'T KEEP IT IN. IT'S RIGHT.
I'M AFRAID. LIKE A BEAST IN A TRAP.
I'M SO AFRAID.

I'M--
KRAK
NOW YOU SEE ME, DON'T YOU?
LANGSTROM...
YOU MURDERED HIM.

THERE WAS A GAP IN HIS SOUL BETWEEN LANGSTROM AND THE MAN-BAT. SO VERY NARROW. BUT I FIT MYSELF WITHIN IT.
WIDENED IT WITH HIS FEAR.
AND I CRAWLED HERE FROM HELL.
NOW I WILL GLUT ON THIS CITY. IT WILL ONLY TAKE A GLIMPSE OF ME TO LET ME ROOT IN YOUR MINDS.
I WILL LAY MY EGGS IN THE TERROR OF CHILDREN, AND THEY WILL HATCH TO SPREAD ACROSS THE EARTH.
THE MORE WHO FEAR ME, THE MORE I SHALL MULTIPLY.
YOU MAY FEAR ME FIRST.
YOU MURDERED HIM.
THUK
HNN--
YOU THINK PAIN WILL--?
A GAP... IN MY... SOUL.
?

SLAM
BUT...
GO BACK...TO THAT GAP.
NO... YOU FEAR.
NO.
NEURGH!
YOU KNOW OF ME NOW.
YOU WILL SPEAK OF ME. EVENTUALLY. AND SOMEONE SHALL FEAR ME.
THAT'S ALL IT WILL TAKE.
SKLURTCH
HEEER-RUUGH!

B-BATMAN?
I DIDN'T LET IT...USE MY FEAR.
I'M...NOT COMING BACK FROM THIS.
NO. I DON'T THINK SO.
IT **LIED.** I'M NOT AN ANIMAL.
A GAP IN MY SOUL... BETWEEN **KIRK** AND **MAN-BAT.**
THERE'S A PART OF ME THAT WAS ALWAYS... **ME.** A MAN.
NO ONE CAN KNOW WHAT HAPPENED. EVEN FRANCINE.
IF SOMEONE KNOWS IT EXISTS... AND THEY **FEAR** IT... IT MIGHT FIND A FOOTHOLD.
IT MIGHT--
KIRK?

HE WAS RIGHT, OF COURSE. NO ONE CAN KNOW. AND NO ONE DOES, EXCEPT FOR THE MAN WAITING IN A GRAVEYARD.
HENCE THE RUSHED FUNERAL. THE LACK OF DIGNITY AND CELEBRATION FOR A MAN WHO PROVED HIMSELF DESERVING OF BOTH.
AND HERE SHE IS NOW. HE HOPED AND DREADED SHE WOULD COME.
FRANCINE LANGSTROM LIVES IN BLÜDHAVEN THESE DAYS. SHE CAME AS SOON AS THE CALL CAME. BATMAN ONLY CALLED THIS MORNING.
SHE DESERVES TO KNOW.
SHE DESERVES TO KNOW HER HUSBAND DIED TO SPARE US UNTOLD HORRORS, KNOWING HIS OWN STORY MUST GO UNTOLD.
SHE DESERVES TO KNOW OF THIS TRULY SELFLESS ACT.
SHE'S A BRAVE WOMAN. PERHAPS SHE WOULD NOT FEAR THE DEMON. SURELY, SHE WOULD NOT TELL ANYONE ELSE.
THE MAN IN THE GRAVEYARD WAITS, NOT KNOWING WHAT HE WILL SAY.
TO BE CONTINUED IN THE PAGES OF DETECTIVE COMICS...

I meet so many young reporters in Gotham City. They always want that one piece of advice that's going to unlock a career for them. I tell them all the same thing.
"It's never the stories you *try* to find that matter…
"…it's the stories that find *you.*"
MR. GOODFELLOW? WHAT ARE THE ODDS?
OH $#@$, DONOVAN. ARE YOU *FOLLOWING* ME?
THE PRESIDENT OF THE GOTHAM TRANSIT AUTHORITY SHOULDN'T REALLY BE SURPRISED TO SEE PEOPLE ON THE SUBWAY, SHOULD HE?
YOU STRIKE ME MORE AS THE "ALWAYS IN A RUSH" TAXI TYPE, DEB.
TAXIS COST MONEY, ELDEN. AND IN CASE YOU HADN'T HEARD, PRINT JOURNALISM ISN'T EXACTLY WHAT IT USED TO BE.
BUT SINCE WE'RE BOTH HERE, *AND* YOU'VE BEEN DUCKING MY CALLS, LET ME ASK YOU…
YOU KEEP TALKING ABOUT *FARE HIKES* AND *SERVICE CUTS.* THAT WOULDN'T HAVE ANYTHING TO DO…
…WITH THE *MILLIONS* RUMORED TO HAVE *VANISHED* FROM THE AGENCY'S PENSION FUND, WOULD IT?
EXCUSE YOU, @#$%?!@$ %$&!

WHY YOU BUMPIN' INTO ME?
GET OUTTA MY FACE, MAN!
BACK UP.
SIGH
LAST STOP! LAST STOP! THIS TRAIN IS NOW OUT OF SERVICE WHILE WE WAIT FOR THE POLICE. EVERYONE OFF.
WHO WOULDN'T WANT TO PAY MORE FOR SERVICE LIKE THIS?
EXPECT DELAYS. IF YOU CAN FIND ALTERNATE TRANSIT TO YOUR DESTINATION, DO SO.
COME ON NOW, ELDEN. CAN I JUST GET ANY COMMENT ABOUT THE FARE HIKES?
OFF THE RECORD?
IF IT HAS TO BE.
THE WHOLE TRANSIT SYSTEM IS A BROKEN, CORRUPT MESS AND NO AMOUNT OF WORK BY YOU OR ME WILL FIX IT. WANNA KNOW WHY?
BECAUSE THIS DAMN CITY GETS THE SERVICES IT DESERVES.
You can always find someone with something to say about

But get a story that speaks to you directly.
HELLO, DAVID? CAN YOU CALL A CAB FOR ME? I'M AT THE 148TH STREET STATION.
YES, I FOUND HIM.
RUSTLE RUSTLE
NO, HE DIDN'T HAVE ANYTHING USEFUL FOR ME...
Or maybe it slips a note in your pocket when you aren't looking.
...BUT I MAY HAVE SOMETHING.
I HAVE TO GO.
WAYNE ENTERPRISES
In Gotham there is a great story around every corner. You just have to listen.

MORGUE
My first editor told me there are multiple ways to get what you need from every source, every lead, and every subject. The trick is figuring them all out.
It took me a few years to learn that I don't need to figure out the other ways, because the first one is *always* money.
IF I'M BEIN' HONEST, THIS IS A REAL UNUSUAL REQUEST, MS. DONOVAN. I'M HOPING YOU HAVE A NEWSPAPER REASON...
...AND THIS ISN'T, LIKE, YOUR *THING.*
NO, *RONALD.* THIS IS DECIDEDLY *NOT* MY THING.
SO. HERE WE ARE...
YES.
...YUP.
LET'S OPEN THEM UP.
I JUST GET CREEPED OUT BY THIS STUFF.
MAYBE YOU SHOULD CONSIDER GETTING A NEW JOB. MY COUSIN SOPHIE SELLS VITAMINS. SHE ALMOST NEVER HAS TO DEAL WITH CORPSES.
NOW OPEN IT UP.

IS THAT...
BANE.
I TOLD YOU AT THE DOOR, THERE'S NOTHING WEIRD GOING ON HERE. YOU SATISFIED?
NOT PARTICULARLY.
SHOW ME THE REST.
I DON'T GET WHAT YOU'RE LOOKING FOR.
NEITHER DO I.
Sometimes, as much as you want a story to come to you, it turns out there's nothing there…
HUH. THAT'S WEIRD.
WHAT'S THAT?
I KNOW SHE WAS HERE. I LOADED HER BODY IN MYSELF.
WHO WAS IT?
ASTRID ARKHAM.
THE ARKHAM KNIGHT.
And sometimes "nothing there" is a good thing.

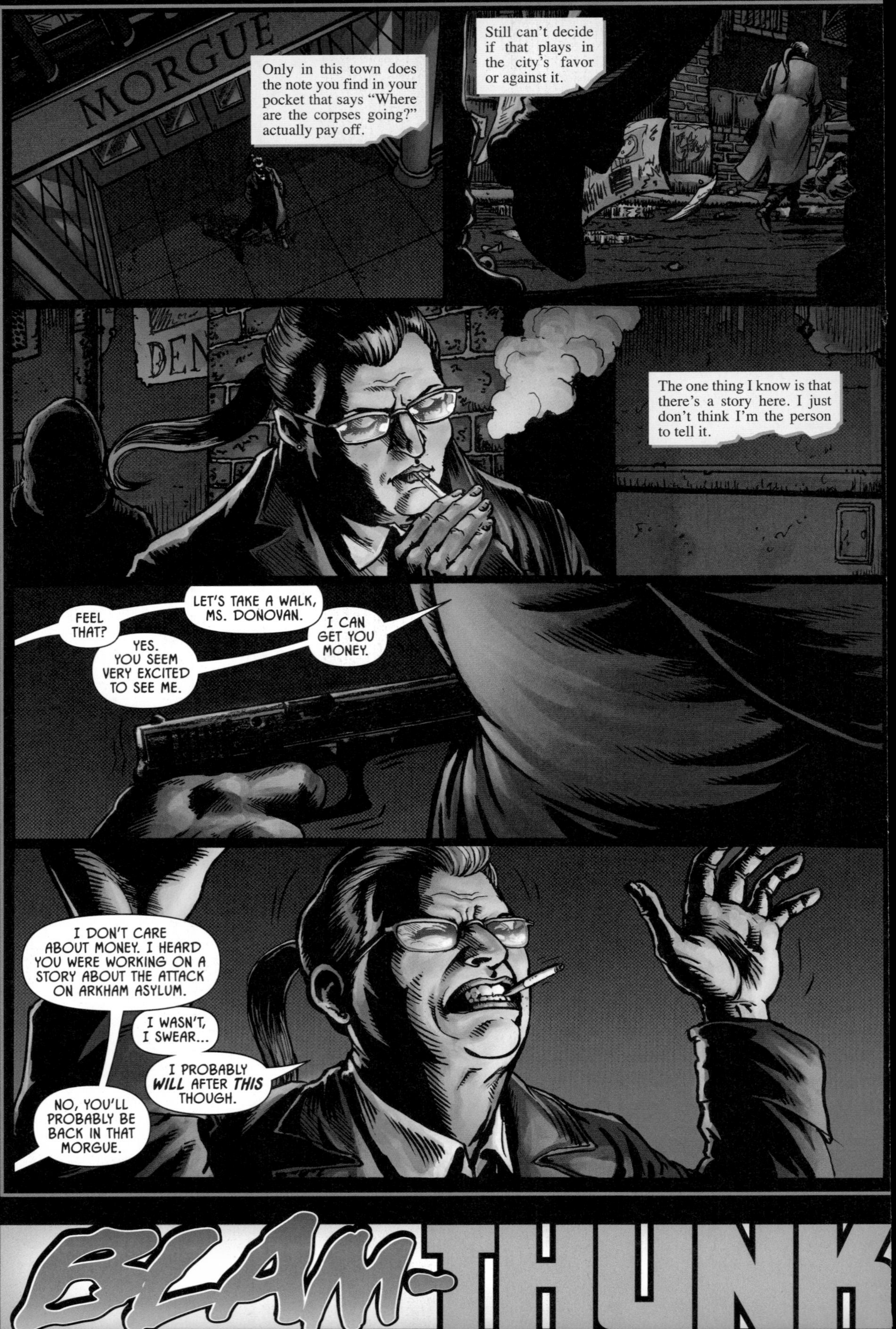
MORGUE
Only in this town does the note you find in your pocket that says "Where are the corpses going?" actually pay off.
Still can't decide if that plays in the city's favor or against it.
The one thing I know is that there's a story here. I just don't think I'm the person to tell it.
FEEL THAT?
LET'S TAKE A WALK, MS. DONOVAN.
YES. YOU SEEM VERY EXCITED TO SEE ME.
I CAN GET YOU MONEY.
I DON'T CARE ABOUT MONEY. I HEARD YOU WERE WORKING ON A STORY ABOUT THE ATTACK ON ARKHAM ASYLUM.
I WASN'T, I SWEAR...
I PROBABLY *WILL* AFTER *THIS* THOUGH.
NO, YOU'LL PROBABLY BE BACK IN THAT MORGUE.
BLAM-THUNK

YOU CAN OPEN YOUR EYES, MS. DONOVAN.
BUT TAKE MY ADVICE. LEAVE THE ARKHAM STORY ALONE.
I JUST HAD TO SAVE YOUR LIFE.
YOU MY EDITOR NOW, BATMAN? BECAUSE I DON'T LIKE IT WHEN STRANGE MEN TELL ME HOW TO DO MY JOB. AND THEY DON'T COME MUCH STRANGER THAN YOU.
WELL, THAT'S YOUR JOB. NOW LET ME DO MINE.
I WON'T WARN YOU AGAIN.
GO HOME.

...AND KEEP THESE COMING. ME AND THE ILLUSTRIOUS VICKI VALE PLAN ON GETTING SLOPPY THIS EVENING.
OOOKAY, DEB. IT WAS A FORTY-DOLLAR CAB RIDE OVER HERE AND MY ALARM CLOCK IS GOING OFF IN FIVE HOURS, SO THIS BETTER BE... I DON'T EVEN KNOW WHAT.
I... WHAT IS THIS?
SOMEONE SLIPPED IT INTO MY POCKET ON THE SUBWAY YESTERDAY MORNING.
THIS IS UNBELIEVABLE.
DEB DONOVAN ON THE SUBWAY?! I DON'T BUY IT.
CUTE.
I WAS GOING TO DRINK THAT--
--OR NOT.
LOOK, DON'T WE JUST ASSUME THIS CAME FROM YOUR AVERAGE GOTHAM CRACKPOT?
I THOUGHT THAT MIGHT BE IT TOO...
...UNTIL SOMEONE TRIED TO MURDER ME AN HOUR AGO.
OH MY GOD. WHAT HAPPENED? ARE YOU OKAY?
OF COURSE I AM. THAT'S WHY I'M DRINKING DOLLAR SHOTS IN A BIKER BAR AT THREE A.M. ON A TUESDAY, VICKI.

A GUY TOLD ME TO STOP CHECKING OUT THE STORY...
THAT'S NOT ALMOST GETTING KILLED--
WHILE HE PRESSED A GUN INTO MY LIVER.
OH.
IT SOUNDS LIKE YOU HAVE *SOMETHING* HERE. BUT THIS ISN'T YOUR USUAL TYPE OF STORY, DEB.
YOU THINK I DON'T KNOW THAT? THAT'S WHY I CALLED YOU.
RIGHT. GOOD. LET ME TAKE THIS NOTE AND GET IT ANALYZED. THEN--
I'M NOT *GIVING* YOU THE STORY, VICKI. I'M *ASKING* FOR ADVICE.
MY ADVICE IS THAT YOU GIVE ME THE STORY.
WOULD YOU GIVE IT TO ME IF THINGS WERE REVERSED?
FAIR ENOUGH. SO WHAT HAPPENED TO THE GUY WITH THE GUN?
BATMAN SHOWED UP AND DID HIS THING.
OH, WOW. THAT'S LUCKY.
IS IT?
YOU... *WANTED* TO BE MURDERED IN AN ALLEY?
I MEAN, IS IT LUCK THAT BATMAN WAS THERE? OR IS IT ALL *CONNECTED?*
CONNECTED TO *WHAT?*
DO I LOOK LIKE I KNOW THAT?!
SLAM
DID BATMAN SPEAK?
YEAH. HE *ALSO* TOLD ME TO STOP CHECKING OUT THE STORY.
HMM... THAT MIGHT BE GOOD ADVICE.
HOW COME WHEN A GUY WITH A GUN SAYS IT YOU SAY, "$@$% THAT, THERE'S A GOOD STORY HERE," BUT WHEN A GUY DRESSED LIKE A GIANT BAT SAYS IT YOU'RE ALL, "YOU SHOULD PROBABLY LISTEN TO HIM"?

"I'VE BEEN COVERING CRIME IN THIS TOWN FOR YEARS, DEB.
"THE ONLY THING I KNOW FOR SURE IS IF HE SAYS SOMETHING, YOU SHOULD PROBABLY LISTEN."
STUPID VICKI VALE. WHAT DOES SHE...
...KNOW?
This story definitely found me.
WHO THE @$%& ARE YOU?!
I SEE YOU GOT MY NOTE.
And it's eating my @#%&$ cereal.
DEB DONOVAN IN
WHAT THE #!$% IS TASK FORCE Z
PART 1
MATTHEW ROSENBERG writer
DARICK ROBERTSON artist
DIEGO RODRIGUEZ colors
ROB LEIGH letters
DAVE WIELGOSZ associate editor
PAUL KAMINSKI editor
TO BE CONTINUED...

Being a reporter takes you to unexpected places.
MORE COFFEE FOR THE LADY AND...
...A BURGER DELUXE, SPAGHETTI AND MEATBALLS, CHICKEN WINGS, AND A CAESAR SALAD FOR... UMM...
YOU.
HUNGRY, HUH?
HOW THOUGHTFUL.
SALAD'S FOR YOU. IT'LL SOAK UP SOME OF THE BOOZE.
DEB DONOVAN IN
WHAT THE #!$% IS
TASK FORCE Z
PART 2
MATTHEW ROSENBERG writer
MAX RAYNOR artist
DIEGO RODRIGUEZ colors
ROB LEIGH letters
DAVE WIELGOSZ associate editor
PAUL KAMINSKI editor
BEN ABERNATHY group editor
PEOPLE ARE STARING.
99¢
I ASKED IF YOU WANTED TO CLEAN YOURSELF UP BEFORE WE LEFT YOUR PLACE.
I DON'T THINK THAT'S WHY THEY'RE STARING.
IT'S GOTHAM. THEY'LL GET USED TO IT.

SO ARE YOU GOING TO TELL ME WHY I'M AT A DINER IN THE MIDDLE OF THE NIGHT...
...WITH THE MASKED CREEP WHO BROKE INTO MY HOUSE?
THAT'S A QUESTION ONLY YOU CAN ANSWER.
THIS WORKS? THE JAMES DEAN ATTITUDE AND THE CREEPY MASK, PEOPLE FIND THIS CUTE?
NO. I DON'T THINK ANYONE THINKS I'M THE CUTE ONE.
MENU
SO WHAT ARE WE TALKING ABOUT... UMM...I DON'T EVEN KNOW WHAT TO CALL YOU?
I TOLD YOU BEFORE. RED HOOD.
KEEP CALM AND EAT PIE
OPEN
I'M NOT CALLING AN ADULT THAT.
WELL, DEB, THEN I GUESS YOU'RE STICKING WITH "MASKED CREEP."
TO ANSWER YOUR OTHER QUESTION, I THINK WE CAN HELP EACH OTHER.
I GET HOW I HELP YOU. I'M CHASING DOWN LEADS AND UNCOVERING THE STORY. HOW EXACTLY DO YOU HELP ME?
IF I'M LUCKY, AT THE END OF THIS I'M NOT DEAD. YOU GET A PULITZER AND A BOOK DEAL WHEN THIS IS OVER. YOU SHOULD BE HAPPY I CONSIDER THAT EQUAL.
SO WHY ALL THIS CLANDESTINE STUFF? THE NOTE IN MY POCKET?
WOULD YOU HAVE CHECKED OUT THE STORY IF IT WASN'T MYSTERIOUS?
AND BREAKING INTO MY HOME?
I NEEDED TO MAKE SURE YOU WERE DOING YOUR HOMEWORK. YOU WERE.

YOU KNOW WHAT? I DON'T NEED THE WEIRD GUY WITH THE BATMAN FETISH SPELL-CHECKING ME. I THINK WE'RE DONE HERE. YOU COME BY ME AGAIN AND I'LL CALL THE POLICE.
OPEN
THAT'S FINE. 315 PONI COURT.
IS THAT SUPPOSED TO MEAN SOMETHING TO ME?
THAT'S VICKI VALE'S ADDRESS. IF YOU DON'T WANT A GREAT STORY, I'M SURE SHE WILL.
IF YOU'RE SO SURE VICKI WILL GO FOR IT, WHY'D YOU COME TO ME?
I LIKE YOUR WRITING BETTER.
OKAY. THAT WORKED. YOU CAN BE MY ANGRY LITTLE SIDEKICK.
THAT DOESN'T ALWAYS TURN OUT GREAT. BUT LET'S GO OVER WHAT YOU KNOW SO FAR.
WELL, WE KNOW ASTRID ARKHAM FAKED HER OWN DEATH.
DO WE? WE KNOW HER BODY ISN'T AT THE MORGUE.
THINK ABOUT IT.
SMART GIRL. WELL-TO-DO. POWERFUL FAMILY. BUT A TROUBLED PAST.
SOME GREASED PALMS AND SOME FORGED SIGNATURES AND SHE HAS A WHOLE NEW LIFE FAR AWAY.
IT'S THE ONLY LOGICAL EXPLANATION.
AGREED...
EXCEPT SHE IS DEAD. I SAW HER BODY.

FIRST OF ALL, WHAT THE @#$&? SECOND, WHAT ARE YOU SAYING? SOMEONE STOLE HER CORPSE?
YES!
ARE YOU ASKING ME?
I HAVE NO IDEA. BUT I TRUST MY PARTNER WILL TELL ME WHEN SHE FINDS OUT.
MEN
A TOWN LIKE THIS HAS A LOT OF USES FOR A CORPSE LIKE HERS...
WHAT?
JUST BECAUSE SHE WAS DEAD DOESN'T MEAN SHE STILL IS.
WHAT?!
EVEN IF SHE IS DEAD, DOESN'T MEAN SHE DIDN'T WALK OUT OF THAT MORGUE HERSELF.
YOU MIGHT START BY ASKING MAYOR NAKANO WHAT PROJECT HALPERIN IS AND WHY IT HAS FULL ACCESS TO HIS CITY'S RESOURCES.
THANKS FOR DINNER.
BYE BYE
CAN I GET YOU ANYTHING ELSE OR JUST THE CHECK?
I... I DON'T THINK I BROUGHT MY WALLET.

When you are *coming up* as a journalist, they don't tell you about the dangerous men breaking into your house or the attempted murders.
MORNING, DEB!
"Being a journalist is fun and rewarding," they say.
EDITORIAL MEETING IN FIVE, PEOPLE.
"You get to talk to all sorts of people."
MA'AM, I'M NOT GONNA TELL YOU AGAIN--
"You get to travel."
EVERYONE LISTEN UP! IT'S TARA'S BIRTHDAY. WE'RE GOING TO PANCHO'S TACOS FOR LUNCH.
"You can make your own hours," they say.
LOOKS LIKE ANOTHER LATE NIGHT, MS. DONOVAN.
"And it feels good to know your work helps people."
YOU DIDN'T HEAR IT FROM ME.
OF COURSE NOT.
IF THIS COMES BACK TO ME, I'LL BE RUINED.

AND YOU'LL MAKE VALE'S OVERTIME-PAY STORY DISAPPEAR, RIGHT?
THAT'S NOT HOW THIS WORKS, MR. ANDERTON. BUT NICE TRY.
HEY, DEB.
YOU BUSY?
NOPE. WHAT'S UP?
I THINK I MIGHT FINALLY BE CRACKING THIS STORY, VICKI.
THAT'S GREAT. WHATCHA GOT?
YOU KNOW MARTIN ANDERTON FROM THE MAYOR'S OFFICE?
OF COURSE. HE'S THE FOCUS OF MY CORRUPTION STORY.
YEAH... HE MIGHT BE AN ANONYMOUS SOURCE NOW INSTEAD.
WHAT DID YOU DO?! DID YOU JUST $@%# ME, DONOVAN?
I HAD TO TRADE WITH HIM. BUT I'LL MAKE IT UP TO YOU.
HE TOLD ME A WHOLE BUNCH OF "WEIRD STUFF" IS ABOUT TO GO DOWN TOMORROW.
WHAT KIND OF "WEIRD STUFF"?
HE DIDN'T KNOW. BUT STAFF ARE BEING MOVED OR TOLD TO TAKE THE DAY OFF. POLICE WERE ALERTED TO SOME SORT OF FEDERAL DRILL DOWNTOWN.
WHAT DOES ALL THIS MEAN?
NO IDEA. BUT HE SAID SOMEONE HIGH UP WAS PAYING OFF ALL THE RIGHT PEOPLE TO MOVE THINGS ALONG QUICKLY AND KEEP THEM QUIET.
THIS COULD BE BIG, DEB. ARE YOU GOING TO MESSAGE YOUR BOY SIDEKICK?
I'LL CHECK IT OUT AND IF IT TURNS OUT TO BE SOMETHING, I'LL TELL HIM...
...OR HE CAN READ ABOUT IT IN MY COLUMN.
HA.

Every time I meet someone who doesn't know what a journalist actually does, it turns out they think we just do *stakeouts* all the time.
This is actually my first. So far it's a lot of wondering if my butt will ever wake up again and trying to figure out if anyone would notice if I peed on the street.
So I think I'm doing it *right.*
GOTHAM MEDICAL EXAMINER
Finally, some movement.
No idea who he is or what he's doing, but I'm considering blowing this whole thing to ask if I can use the bathroom.
AUTHORIZED PERSONNEL ONLY
Well, this definitely just became *something.* Maybe Red Hood was right. These don't *look* like good guys…
But neither does he, I suppose.
I really hope he's wrong and they aren't stealing corpses… ***or helping them escape.***

KA-CHUK
AAAHH!
VERY SUBTLE, DEB. BUT YOU AREN'T ACTUALLY SUPPOSED TO LET EVERYONE KNOW YOU'RE ON A STAKEOUT.
FIRST TIME?
NO!
WHAT ARE YOU DOING HERE? DID YOU FOLLOW ME?
SHOULDN'T DRINK COFFEE ON A STAKEOUT. MAKES YOU HAVE TO PEE.
I GOT WORRIED WHEN YOU FORGOT TO GET IN TOUCH.
I JUST FOUND OUT ABOUT THIS!
ONLY HAD TIME TO TELL YOUR EDITOR AND VICKI VALE, BUT NOT TIME TO LEAVE ME A NOTE AT THE DROP SPOT? IS THAT IT?
ARE YOU... DID YOU TAP MY PHONE?
YES.
DON'T LIE TO ME. I CAN FIND OUT--
I SAID YES. I PUT A BUG ON YOUR PHONE THAT MORNING ON THE SUBWAY.

YOU THINK I WOULD STAGE THAT WHOLE FIGHT JUST TO PUT A NOTE IN YOUR POCKET? I HAD TO MAKE SURE I COULD TRUST YOU.
OH MY GOD.
I CAN'T, BY THE WAY.
NO. **LOOK.**
THEY'RE ***STEALING DEAD PEOPLE!***
WHY WOULD ANYONE ***STEAL DEAD PEOPLE?!***
SO IT SEEMS.
LET ME GO ASK.
WAIT!
THERE'S STILL A STORY HERE. SOMETHING BIG IS GOING ON. THIS ISN'T JUST THEM.
SO?
DON'T YOU WANT TO KNOW WHO THEY'RE WORKING FOR? WHAT THEY'RE DOING?
YOU CAN ASK THEM WHEN I'M DONE.
STAY IN THE CAR.

Every good reporter hits a point in their career where they have to make a decision. Do they chase the story and risk seeing people get hurt? Or do they intervene and risk losing the story?
I don't want to lose this story.
But I also don't want to watch a murder.
HELLO, POLICE? MY NAME IS DEB DONOVAN--
WACK
MA'AM?
MA'AM, ARE YOU THERE?
911
TO BE CONTINUED...

WHAT THE HELL DID YOU DO?
SHE WAS WITH THE RED HOOD.
What the @#$& did I get myself into?
THIS LADY LOOK LIKE A SUPERHERO TO YOU?
NO, BUT WE CAN'T JUST LET--
LOOK OUT!
WHACK
NO! STAY BACK!
SLAM

I always assumed that if you spend enough time covering these masked vigilantes, that you just get used to it.
It becomes your new normal.
I TOLD YOU TO STAY OUT OF THIS.
Now I realize that no one should ever get used to this. This *isn't normal.*
ROS
wines
LIQUOR
I...I ***WAS*** GOING TO.
BUT ***HE*** DRAGGED ME BACK INTO IT.
YOU KNOW HIM, RIGHT?
BRAKKA BRAKKA BRAKKA

YES, I KNOW HIM.
WUPWUPWUP
THIS IS THE GOTHAM POLICE.
GET OFF THE VEHICLE AND LIE FACEDOWN ON THE GROUND!
WE HAVE TO GET YOU OUT OF HERE. YOU CAN'T BE HERE WHEN THE POLICE ARRIVE.
WHY NOT?!
KRAK
TRUST ME.
WHAT ABOUT THE RED HOOD?
HE CAN TAKE CARE OF HIMSELF.

I'M NOT LEAVING. IT'S MY JOB TO--
HEY! WHAT THE--
$%&#@&#!
THIS IS MUCH BIGGER THAN YOU KNOW, MS. DONOVAN. IT WOULD BE BETTER IF YOU DON'T RUN THE STORY.
I'M NOT WORRIED ABOUT MY SAFETY.
I CAN TELL.
THESE PEOPLE YOU'RE WRITING ABOUT ARE DANGEROUS. IF YOUR STORY COMES OUT, THEY'LL VANISH.
THEY WON'T STOP THOUGH. YOUR STORY WILL JUST MAKE THEM HARDER TO CATCH.
THE HARDER YOU MAKE MY JOB, THE MORE PEOPLE GET HURT.
DON'T MAKE MY JOB HARDER.
YEAH, ABOUT THAT...HOW DO I GET DOWN FROM HERE?

WHO ARE YOU WORKING FOR?!
KRAK
STOP OR WE WILL OPEN FIRE, &@%$#!
I'LL DEAL WITH HIM.
IT'S TIME TO GO.
YOU CAN GO, BATMAN. I'M SEEING THIS THROUGH.

IT'S OVER!
NO!
YOU LEAVE NOW OR YOU DON'T LEAVE.
NOT YOUR CASE. NOT YOUR CALL.
GPD POLICE
POLICE
PUM
DAMMIT. I CAN'T PROTECT YOU FROM THIS.
YOU THINK I DON'T HAVE WAYS OF MAKING YOU TALK?
GO @#$& YOURSELF.
KLIK
OH NO.

THOOM
FEDERAL AGENTS! NOBODY MOVE!
POLICE
WE HAVE JURISDICTION. YOU CAN CALL IT IN WITH YOUR DIRECTOR IF YOU NEED TO. WE ARE ON ASSIGNMENT HERE.
POLICE
POLICE
POLICE
WHAT ABOUT THE RED HOOD? WE HAVE A WARRANT FOR--
POLICE
HE *IS* OUR ASSIGNMENT.
FBI
DEPARTMENT OF INVESTIGATION
FBI

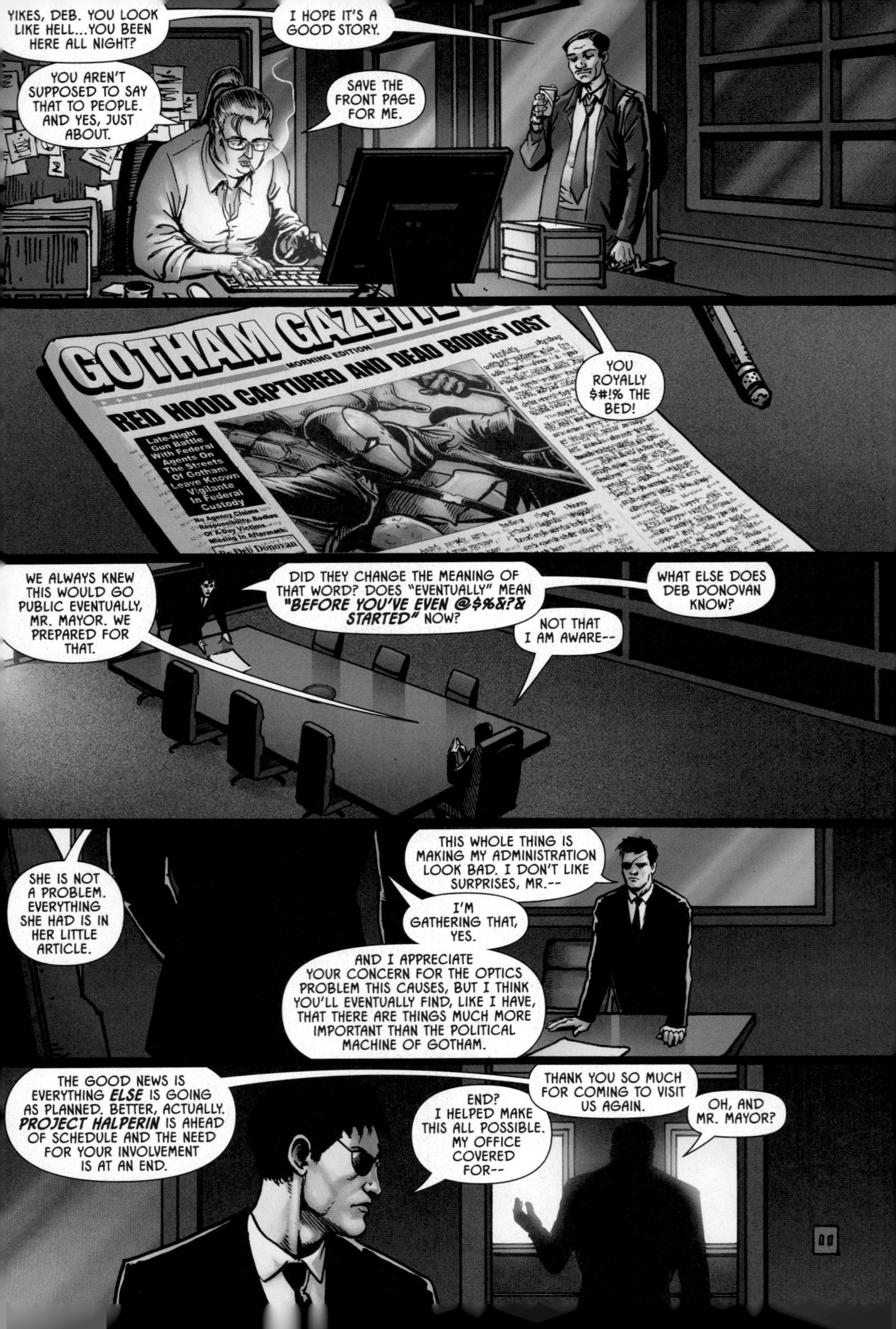
YIKES, DEB. YOU LOOK LIKE HELL...YOU BEEN HERE ALL NIGHT?
YOU AREN'T SUPPOSED TO SAY THAT TO PEOPLE. AND YES, JUST ABOUT.
I HOPE IT'S A GOOD STORY.
SAVE THE FRONT PAGE FOR ME.
GOTHAM GAZETTE
MORNING EDITION
RED HOOD CAPTURED AND DEAD BODIES LOST
Late-Night Gun Battle With Federal Agents On The Streets Of Gotham Leave Known Vigilante In Federal Custody
No Agency Claims Responsibility; Bodies Of A-Day Victims Missing In Aftermath
By Deb Donovan
YOU ROYALLY $#!% THE BED!
WE ALWAYS KNEW THIS WOULD GO PUBLIC EVENTUALLY, MR. MAYOR. WE PREPARED FOR THAT.
DID THEY CHANGE THE MEANING OF THAT WORD? DOES "EVENTUALLY" MEAN "BEFORE YOU'VE EVEN @$%&?& STARTED" NOW?
WHAT ELSE DOES DEB DONOVAN KNOW?
NOT THAT I AM AWARE--
SHE IS NOT A PROBLEM. EVERYTHING SHE HAD IS IN HER LITTLE ARTICLE.
THIS WHOLE THING IS MAKING MY ADMINISTRATION LOOK BAD. I DON'T LIKE SURPRISES, MR.--
I'M GATHERING THAT, YES.
AND I APPRECIATE YOUR CONCERN FOR THE OPTICS PROBLEM THIS CAUSES, BUT I THINK YOU'LL EVENTUALLY FIND, LIKE I HAVE, THAT THERE ARE THINGS MUCH MORE IMPORTANT THAN THE POLITICAL MACHINE OF GOTHAM.
THE GOOD NEWS IS EVERYTHING ELSE IS GOING AS PLANNED. BETTER, ACTUALLY. PROJECT HALPERIN IS AHEAD OF SCHEDULE AND THE NEED FOR YOUR INVOLVEMENT IS AT AN END.
END? I HELPED MAKE THIS ALL POSSIBLE. MY OFFICE COVERED FOR--
THANK YOU SO MUCH FOR COMING TO VISIT US AGAIN.
OH, AND MR. MAYOR?

"YOU CAN TRUST ME, SIR."
HELLO, JASON. I ASSUME OTHER THAN A FEW MINOR CUTS AND CONTUSIONS FROM YOUR CAPTURE, YOU HAVE NO COMPLAINTS?
FIVE STARS. WOULD RECOMMEND TO ALL MY FRIENDS.
I GET THE JOKE, BUT I FEEL I SHOULD REMIND YOU THAT YOU NO LONGER HAVE ANY FRIENDS, JASON.
YOU DO KNOW YOU'RE A WANTED MAN, CORRECT? YOU'VE HURT A LOT OF PEOPLE, KILLED PEOPLE EVEN. THERE AREN'T A LOT OF LAWS YOU DIDN'T BREAK.
BUT MY UNDERSTANDING IS YOU'RE BACK IN GOTHAM TRYING TO CHANGE THAT STORY. LOCAL BOY MAKES GOOD, YES?
THAT STARTS HERE, JASON. YOUR REDEMPTION ARC.
LET ME GET THOSE CHAINS OFF YOU.
KLIK KLIK
IF I'M NOT UNDER ARREST...WHAT IS THIS?
IT'S A JOB INTERVIEW.
WHAT'S THE JOB?

DEB DONOVAN IN
WHAT THE #!$% IS
TASK FORCE Z
FINALE
MATTHEW ROSENBERG writer
DARICK ROBERTSON artist
DIEGO RODRIGUEZ colors
ROB LEIGH letters
DAVE WIELGOSZ associate editor
PAUL KAMINSKI editor
BATMAN created by Bob Kane with Bill Finger.
I'M PUTTING TOGETHER A TEAM AND THEY'RE DYING TO MEET YOU...
TO BE CONTINUED IN THE PAGES OF TASK FORCE Z #1!
THAT'S WHERE THINGS GET COMPLICATED.

VARIANT COVER
GALLERY

Detective Comics #1040 variant cover by LEE BERMEJO

Detective Comics #1042 variant cover by LEE BERMEJO

Detective Comics #1043 variant cover by LEE BERMEJO

Detective Comics #1043 variant cover by KAEL NGU

Detective Comics #1044 variant cover by LEE BERMEJO

Detective Comics #1045 variant cover by LEE BERMEJO

Batman Secret Files: The Huntress #1 variant cover by RICCARDO FEDERICI

AFTERWORD
BY DAN MORA

I don't think I can find the right words to express the emotion and the feeling of professional achievement that this opportunity has meant for me. Being a part of the team that brings this character to life has been a surreal experience. To be able to contribute my vision of the hero, to transmit my tastes and preferences in the small details, to illustrate Gotham's iconic architecture and reimagine the vigilante's classic poses in his strategic gargoyle pose at night is something I never thought I would get to do, and something I am immensely grateful for. Being a part of this legacy of artists who have kept the myth alive is a great honor, one that I hope I can live up to.

Batman was the first superhero that resonated with me. I remember my dad buying me a Batman costume, and I wouldn't take it off. It made me feel that I was more than a little boy with his insecurities; it gave me courage and nurtured my imagination. Later, other heroes came, but none like the Bat. He awoke my interest in drawing and fantasy, and since then, has been an important part of my artistic life and now of my professional life.

DAN MORA,
JANUARY 2022

Character sketches by DAN MORA

Cover sketches by DAN MORA

A

B

C

A

B

C

D

A

B

C

D

E

B

Page layouts by **DAN MORA**

1

2

3

4

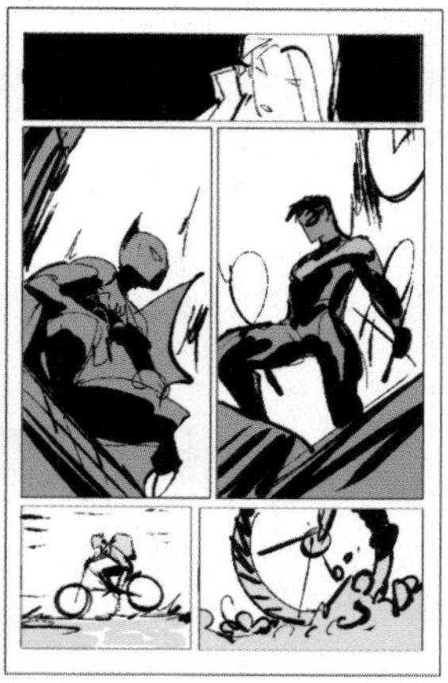

5

6

7

8

9

10

11

12

Page layouts by **DAN MORA**

DETECTIVE COMICS SPECIAL FEATURETTE:
MR. WORTH

ROLAND

Full Name:
Roland Worth

Occupation:
Businessman, steel industry

Powers:
Above-average size/strength

Known Affiliates:
Wife (unnamed), Molly Worth (daughter, deceased), Sarah Worth (daughter, deceased)

Stats:
Eight feet tall, extremely wealthy, and connected in Gotham City

WORTH

Bio:
Roland Worth "helped build half of Gotham" with his steel business. The good times ended when his daughter Molly died of complications from a congenital heart defect...and worsened when his last remaining child, Sarah, was found murdered and Bruce Wayne implicated.

Now Roland aligns himself with the likes of the Penguin and other gangsters in Gotham to take his revenge on those he believes took so much from him.

AT SARAH WORTH'S FUNERAL

LOSING HIS FIRST DAUGHTER, MOLLY

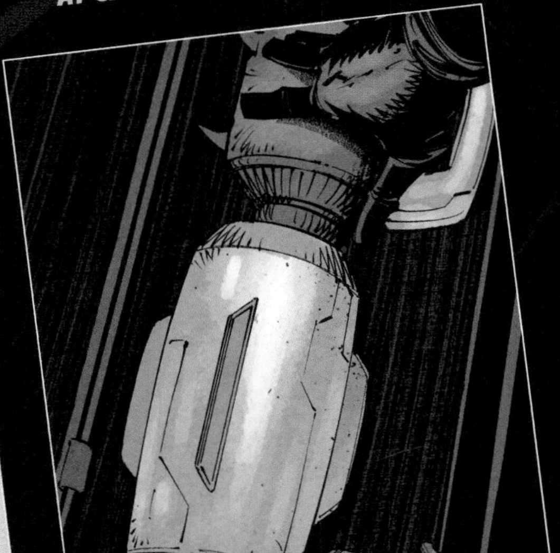

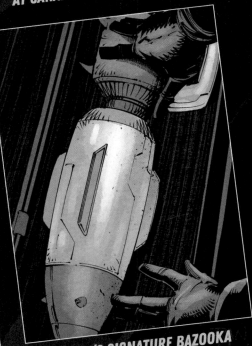

WORTH'S SIGNATURE BAZOOKA

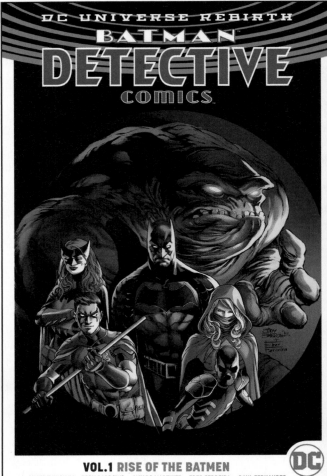

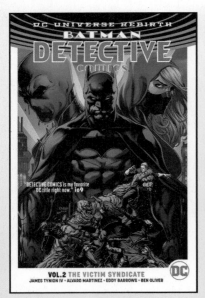